AF442944

वक्रतुण्ड महाकाय सूर्यकोटि समप्रभ ।
निर्विघ्नं कुरु मे देव सर्वकार्येषु सर्वदा ॥

Vakratunda Mahakaya, Surya Koti Samaprabaha
Nirvighnam Kurumedeva Sarva Karyeshu Sarvada

"Greetings to the one who has a curved trunk, and an immense body, the one who illuminates the glow of millions of Suns, and to the one who eliminates obstacles of a common man. May he bless all our endeavors and remove obstacles from our path"

Pic courtesy: thestonestudio.in

How to be The Happiest APE

Master the Science and Art of **consistency** to a life of **contentment** in just 3 weeks

SOURABH DE

CRACK THE SECRET OF THE APE™ TRIANGLE

Copyright © Sourabh De 2023
All Rights Reserved.

ISBN 979-8-89026-944-7

This book has been published with all efforts taken to make the material error-free after the consent of the author. However, the author and the publisher do not assume and hereby disclaim any liability to any party for any loss, damage, or disruption caused by errors or omissions, whether such errors or omissions result from negligence, accident, or any other cause.

While every effort has been made to avoid any mistake or omission, this publication is being sold on the condition and understanding that neither the author nor the publishers or printers would be liable in any manner to any person by reason of any mistake or omission in this publication or for any action taken or omitted to be taken or advice rendered or accepted on the basis of this work. For any defect in printing or binding the publishers will be liable only to replace the defective copy by another copy of this work then available.

There are only two types of people. The ones who would eat the tastiest dish first, and the others who would save it for the last.

Advance Praise for the Book

"Sourabh De not only produces catchy titles, but he produces catchy content too. We are human Apes. But this book is about the APE triangle of achievement, potential and expectation. Happiness is a term difficult to pin down, and philosophers, religious leaders and social scientists have tried to understand it. Our texts talk of equilibrium (*samya*) between everything, the three *gunas* of *sattva*, *rajas* and *tamas*, and the *purusharthas* of *dharma, artha, kama* and *moksha*. Whatever be the definition of happiness, disequilibrium and dissonance between A, P and E will lead to unhappiness. In an engaging style and with wonderful illustrations and charts, Sourabh De has written a self-help book with a difference. The instructions may seem to be simple, but it is the simple that is not practised. If readers imbibe some of the lessons, individuals will be happier, and so will humanity. There is no escape from APE."

– Dr. Bibek Debroy (Author, Scholar and Chairman of the Economic Advisory Council to the Prime Minister of India)

"After his engaging first book *Time Travel: To the edge of history*, Sourabh De is back with another thought-provoking book, which will encourage you to take a fresh look at the choices you make in life, including the effort you put into every task, and the possible outcomes. In other words, it's all about prioritizing."

– Ms. Nirupama Kotru (Senior Civil Servant)

Table of Contents

Part B
The Mechanics of the Story

Part C
The Journey Ahead

**Part D
The Bottomline**

**Part E
3 Weeks to Happiness**

A Token of Gratitude, Only for You

Thank you for choosing my book.

It means a lot to me as I continue my journey of sharing the knowledge and wisdom gathered from the stalwarts of the scientific community as well as the hundreds of coaching clients, mentors, students, professional colleagues and the wise men and women I crossed path with.

Reading this page, you must be wondering what the book holds for you. Let me assure you that every word in it is a testimony to what I have gone through and tested over thousands of times. The intense truth I have discovered about success and happiness is distilled in the following pages. I live by it every moment and wish each one of us out there gets to try the approaches mentioned.

That I would consider the biggest success for this book, if even a single soul can turn around their life and find true happiness.

You can help me in this mission by being one of the first.

And to appreciate your gesture, I humbly invite you to join my website community at *www.sourabhde.com*. I have some special tools, templates, blogs, and stories to engage you, while we walk together in the journey of becoming 'The Happiest APE'.

See you,

– **Sourabh**

Preface

'Why' to be the happiest APE?

This book is about the age-old saying, Time is Money and how our choices, and only our choices, decide where we are in our Happiness Journey.

I experienced that when I decided to write my first book, "Time Travel: To the Edge of History".

I gave it just a 30% chance of success. Prior to that, I had never written anything longer than 5 pages (except, of course, my mandatory master's thesis in Pharmaceutical Sciences).

But soon, it turned out to be a true labour of love, and certainly not easy at the beginning. I crunched about 400 words a day. That's about 30-45 minutes per day. Some days less, other days imperfect, but every day a little.

And 366 days later, I was holding a 450-page long History-Adventure-Travelogue. The end result astounds me even to this date.

That personal feat and the over-the-top validation, curiosity, and praise it generated from readers and friends got me thinking.

How did I pull it through? What were the reasons I could meet this daunting goal?

What behaviours, thoughts, and actions work for me? Are those repeatable?

Are those applicable to others? Can those be applied to other fields of life?

Would those eventually make me a contented person?

What is the ONE thing I choose that would continue to give me that kind of success and fulfilment?

To put things to the test and dispel any doubts, I got down to researching. The approach was understanding how seemingly big and daunting goals need not be met in totality and in one go.

Fast forward to today; the book you are holding in your hand right now is a material outcome of that research into our relationship with Time, Choice, Decisions, and Outcomes.

The research and fieldwork have been a roller coaster. But as someone who deals with people and lots of them in my day job, these conversations came in handy. My colleagues, coaching clients, and students gave firsthand survey responses and testimonials.

The difficult part, though, was to distil the numerous research articles on the psychology of human behaviour and the biological basis of things like satisfaction, contentment, and happiness.

What started emerging was a theme that was never the prime focus, to begin with. It helped me coin several terms, one of them being 'Super-habit'. The other terms, like PAD goals, APE™ Triangle (and similar Time-Money graphs), go on to highlight the fundamentals of our life choices and the rights and wrongs in the pursuit of goal fulfilment and happiness.

The book's essence mimics the ancient Chinese proverb by Sun Tzu: *"The more you sweat in peace, the less you bleed in war"*.

You would be realising that the four fictional characters whose lives have been put on display are not that fictional after all. We will find snatches of them in us. Viraj, Romel, Karishma, and Aneela show how their choices and decisions take them on different trajectories, and yet each can find a way to be back on track.

They show why it is as much important to KNOW your true goals as it is to prioritise meeting them slowly and steadily. Priority first is the first priority.

It is now hardwired in my brain as to how not to fall prey to easy choices and do stuff consistently. It has helped me overcome some of the most difficult moments in my life. Be it my parents' grave illnesses, my own personal health goals, the pursuit of creating something new out of nothing, and the constant endeavor to codify the real 'Template for Happiness'.

My first book and now this second one is an outcome of all the above concepts and experimentation. And all that while working full-time in the corporate sector and pursuing my other interests in Astronomy, History, Archeology, Wildlife, Fitness, Travel, and Coaching students and young professionals.

After reading the synopsis, one of my reviewers asked me why this book's concepts should stand out. After all, there are so many other books out there talking about habits endlessly.

You would know when you go through it that the book doesn't ask us to build 'n' number of habits. It instead suggests how we need only ONE habit that will open the doors to any habit whatsoever. Essentially, what is the Master key to any habit, goal, fulfilment, and happiness in the world?

My attempt has been to live the proverb, *"Give a man a fish, and you feed him for a day, teach him to fish, and you feed him for a lifetime"*.

This book is about learning to fish for that Super-habit through tools, techniques, tips, and templates.

I think he agrees since he is the one who eventually agreed to write the Foreword to the book.

However, we have our arguments on my claim that it was because of the Super-habit of Consistency that I ran a distance equivalent to Delhi to Mumbai and back.

The jury is still out on that.

Foreword

In the last couple of decades, humans have had unprecedented access to physical and digital resources. With that has come a plethora of options, which all seem attractive and just right, and sometimes too good to be true.

What does the average human mind do, then? How does it choose not the most attractive but the most correct option? How do those choices define the outcomes? How do those outcomes define the future trajectory of the decisionmaker?

The distractions of the modern-day options have done more harm and created more confusion than we bargained for.

When I think of my own life, which has been fairly productive and satisfying so far, I can only thank my lucky stars for the lack of options I had in my formative years.

But for the youth and the middle-aged generation today, the challenge is far bigger. Even for someone like me, I hope that life should be far simpler with less to choose from.

The book written by Sourabh De focuses precisely on simplifying the pursuit of better choices and happiness.

The book takes a diagnostic approach and narrows it down to a single all-encompassing habit or trait. It has been called a **Super-habit** and allows everyone to master the art of building good habits and shunning the bad ones. The tools, diagrams, and tips are extremely valuable and unique.

Interestingly the book doesn't speak so much about specific habits as it does about satisfaction/happiness/contentment (more than 100 times) and Choice and Consistency (200 times).

This deliberate focus on choices drives our personal happiness, and the critical trait called consistency sustains our level of happiness.

I found this phrase particularly insightful regarding making tough choices in life.

"There are only two types of people. The ones who would eat the tastiest dish first and the others who would save it for the last".

As one engages with the chapters, it becomes clear that consistency defines the Quality of Life and makes life worth living and each day looking forward to. It's a life skill. The good news is that consistency is a trait that can be developed and is perhaps the most useful trait one could ever ask for.

In one of the chapters, it is mentioned that *"Consistency is the mother of habits and the grandmother of results".* I couldn't agree more. In fact, the book successfully dissociates Motivation and Goal Attainment. It puts consistency above all.

I particularly like the example of a matchstick and candle to explain that.

Holistically, the book is about our choices and learning to accept the outcome of those. It is about what we do consistently shaping us and shaping our future. We often end up calling it our destiny and a function of luck, whereas it is indeed what we have chosen to think about and act on consistently.

The concepts of Time=Money and Accumulation, be it disposable time, resources, choices, health, and outcomes, are all linked with the true goals that we should pursue. The book lays down a step-by-step approach on diagnosing whether what we think should be our goals are indeed true or not. If we pursue the wrong goals, we will be off track for a long time.

The book also helps codify a template for that diagnosis, the decision tree for right and wrong choices, prioritisation, and how the simple trait of consistency alone can take one closer to happiness.

The book is surely going to be an endless source of strength, confidence, foresight, and happiness, for whosoever spends some time on it, irrespective of age and social standing. The concepts and examples are deep and will stick for a lifetime.

– Dr. Anand Ranganathan
Author and Scientist
New Delhi
7th September 2023

PART A

The Story

1. The Meaning of the Journey

I learned that a prosperous life is a productive life, and that productivity leads to a smile of satisfaction.

– John Soforic

Perched on the neem tree, the crow was at its cacophonic best as Karishma paced up and down on her balcony. She was talking to her web designer, who just confirmed that her website is now live, and she should immediately check that and start sending the link to all her followers on social media.

She really liked the look and feel and already saw the visitor count on the website spiking. Also, the number of clicks on her book is soaring. She started getting instant purchase notifications on her cell phone.

She hadn't even started seeing the congratulatory messages and texts yet. Her hands trembled as she tentatively sat down in the gently swaying hammock, still wondering what hit her.

Bits of the confetti strewn around created micro-tornados in the corner of the balcony. It's been a wonderful 42nd birthday just a couple of days back which turned out to be more interesting than the ones she had in her teens. She had launched her debut book that day, with friends, family, and colleagues gushing over her achievement.

She wished hard that all this wouldn't turn out to be a dream. After all, this is what she always wanted to do. A smile came up on her face. She picked up her 'always-go-to' book ('Tales to Live by', the translated work by the Sufi mystic Rumi) from the shelf and returned to the balcony garden, pinching herself.

Just then, a loud buzz woke her up as her hand snapped to knock off the glass of water on the nightstand. It was indeed a dream!

After a nanosecond of disappointment, her smile, a big smile came back. *'It's been indeed a wonderful life'*, she thought aloud, *'just as it was meant to be'*. With many ups and downs, heartbreaks, and ecstasy, of longing and belonging, of losing and finding oneself back. Especially when she met Atul and lost her first child in the womb.

And how could she forget Atul's job loss during the recession? Everything was thrown under the bus. But then, how did things turn around? Destiny? Will? Perspective?

Whatever, she kept lying on the bed, happily forcing herself to relive those moments and the trying times.

There was contentment in the air. She now has enough time, a decent amount of disposable bank balance, and tons guilt-free satisfaction for her life stage.

That feeling of being immensely lucky overwhelmed her every day. Was it her sense of ease with everything around her or the material comfort and security of having enough time and money?

Whatever it was, it seemed to be how a wise person would describe satisfaction or contentment in a more refined manner.

Was it always like that? Far from it.

By the time she was 32, she constantly juggled between keeping a job, a personal life, a home, and whatnot.

Then one day, the **Time-Money equation** started making sense to her. It couldn't have been earlier or later. That was the perfect moment when the equation jumped out of the wall.

The first time she read about the concept was when she was an intern with a Pharmaceutical Marketing company. It didn't cut much ice, then. She was not ready for that key piece of wisdom and common sense.

The fact that the same company later offered her a job convinced her that she couldn't go wrong and didn't need any canned advice from anyone.

However, after three eventful and socially charged years at a 'dream job', many nagging issues mushroomed, and there were too many distractions. Though she was dealing with them instinctively, almost robotically, it left her perennially bored and sleepless.

It took her a couple of more years to step back and realise and reestablish her relationship with 'Time'. And, of course, she had a few helping hands. A senior colleague in her team, who was a certified coach, mentored her for over 6 months. And she let that happen, made that investment. It was an investment not in money but in time.

But wait! Are these 2 different things… money and time?

She recalled her dilemma as she lazily wallowed in the cosy November bed. Her intern days came rushing to her, and so did the conversations around 'Benjamin Franklin' and his 'Time is Money' phrase.

Reminiscing about those, she finally stepped out of bed to fix a mint tea. It was a Wednesday, and she was taking a mid-week off from her 'Teach the World' classes. Atul was at his hometown to meet some ageing relatives. And Naina was at her residential school, 45 km away.

The next week was going to be super exciting. It would mean a culmination of something great and perhaps the beginning of something greater. She heaved a sigh.

She had been in touch with many of her friends from college and the office circle. Most have had very predictable lifelines. However, there are 3 people whose lives played out in great detail before her. Each one is unique, and each one is filled with lessons.

> **Time is more valuable than money. You can get more money, but you cannot get more time.**

2. Three Lives and Five Elements of Nature

Look at a day when you are supremely satisfied at the end. It's not a day when you lounge around doing nothing; it's when you've had everything to do, and you've done it.

– Margaret Thatcher

The lives of those three people proved to be the biggest lessons for Karishma in the subsequent years. She could very clearly recall the many conversations over her many years of association with them.

They were Viraj, Romel, and Aneela.

The Composed Viraj

Viraj was one composed human. Always counting and thinking before opening his mouth or his wallet. He was the one who would be the first person to log in and last to log out, crossing all the t's and dotting all the i's in every email and text message.

He had carved out a decent and safe career for himself. And his clarity made him settle down for a low-maintenance family life. For the 2 kids, their father and mother were playing similar roles, and one could take the place of the other at any time.

Regarding resources, the couple seemed to be ok, with Preeti, his wife, holding on to a teaching job in a play school, allowing them to spend and splurge occasionally. Viraj did harbour a feeling that he should've taken the plunge and shifted to another city when the opportunity had come about 10 years back. This feeling comes along whenever he spends hours and days planning the international vacation his kids have fancied.

But then, he consoled himself. Money alone can't buy the peace of mind that he has today. And all the time he can spend almost every day with the kids.

Karishma had known Viraj as a neighbour while growing up in a modest government housing society in Delhi. Over the years, she had always felt at ease in Viraj's company until the shades of regret and 'what ifs' would surface in his conversations. But that never stopped them from catching up every few months with family and reminiscing about the years gone by.

The Super Smart Romel

Then there was Romel, the superstar heartthrob. He was from the same college where Karishma also passed out from. In fact, Karishma had taught Romel in his 2nd year and when she was pursuing her master's degree.

He was simply unstoppable, overflowing with confidence and energy. Sometimes a disproportionate amount of risk-taking behaviour would see him finish way ahead of the competition.

Later, the structured corporate life seemed too easy and predictable to him. By the time he was 28, he had beaten the company's appraisal system 3 times and made presentations to his CEO and external shareholders. He had also pocketed several media bytes by the time he turned 30. Everyone predicted him to be the next CEO, provided he didn't get bored before that.

As if destined, he jumped the queue again to prove how unpredictable he was. In the next 4 years, he raised millions and created and sold startups like cookies. The rush he felt was unfathomable. His name would be flashed on business channels every few weeks.

Karishma learned more about his trail-blazing runs when she met his wife at a college reunion a year back. He was then recovering from knee and slipped disc surgeries he had to undergo 3 times in 6 months. For the first time, his wife mentioned words like health, stress, settling down, planning, or perhaps adopting a kid, and such 'mundane' problems.

She said Romel wanted to go slow now and do something on his own and not only for the investors. He had enough money to last more than a lifetime, but now there's very little 'Time' left.

These conversations with Rakhi, Romel's wife, got Karishma thinking about Aneela.

The Mercurial Aneela

Quite the opposite of Viraj and Romel in more than many ways.

Aneela was someone who would be called a live wire in any circle. Intelligent, witty, with an ability to strike up a conversation anywhere with anyone.

Notwithstanding her qualification, her ability to socialise and create a great first impression helped her tremendously in her first few years of corporate life. It widened her network both personally and professionally. It allowed her access to the best-known social circuits both online and offline.

Karishma 'lost touch' when Aneela deliberately shied away from her friends and social circles and showed visible signs of cynicism about her surroundings.

And just like that, Aneela went off the air, moving to a small town to apparently save money and recover lost time. Life, according to her, had dealt a severe blow, and she was on a recovery trip; '…to rebuild my life…' she said in her last Instagram post.

'What on Earth was happening with these 3 lives?' Karishma thought as she stepped into her balcony garden as a couple of squirrels were competing (or were they celebrating their exploits) from the Fig tree.

Looks like there are millions out there, like Viraj, Romel, and Aneela, who are in a constant tug-of-war with the 'elements of nature,' whether it is our jobs or life in general.

Karishma pondered those a bit more in relation to what we can control and what controls us. What is the common denominator that plays out right in front of our eyes every moment?

What is that single most important thing we 'can' and 'should' measure as we hurtle down the path of our life journeys?

Time isn't the main thing; it's the only thing.
– Miles Davis

The Five Elements of Nature, or are there more…?

In the ancient Indian texts, there is a concept of *Panchamahabhutas*, which essentially proposes that all kinds of matter in the universe are made up of Earth, Water, Fire, Wind, and Space.

Obviously, these are not the classic 'elements' that have been described as per chemistry. However, in simple terms, let's assume these are the natural building blocks around us that we can perceive, touch, and feel.

To a small extent, we can also control certain aspects of these.

But then there are several other dimensions around us that can also be considered building blocks, hence elements.

Many would argue these to be a matter of philosophy and deep observation through cultural practices for millennia.

Accordingly, the elements could be numbered from the basic 5 to as many as 24, including Time, Light, Force, and so on.

The stories of Viraj, Romel, and Aneela are of their journeys alongside the many elements of nature. The 5 basic ones (Earth, Water, Fire,

Wind, and Space) and 'Time' in the pursuit of greater access to the trappings of the material world. Should we then call it the pursuit of access to resources or, perhaps simplistically, money? Let's hold on to that thought for some time.

Not only mathematically, but also metaphorically, let's break down some of the key elements:

- 'Space' is where all this drama has been unfolding since time immemorial; then, of course, 'Time', the enigmatic element which we can't for sure say whether it flows or is still. Perhaps we, the observer, circle around it or flit by.
- 'Money' or access or resources, whatever you call it. And finally,
- 'Satisfaction' or contentment or simply said, 'sustained state of happiness'.

We should appreciate that there is no single or simple way of describing these elements of nature. A scientist, a commoner, and a philosopher would view these differently. And none is wrong. After all, everything we do, and experience can be interpreted differently by different people. And so is the case with whatever happens to us on our life journeys.

Nevertheless, all are important and point to the fact that the elements of nature are extremely complex, and therefore, we as humans should attempt to grasp whatever little is in our control and leave the rest to the interplay of the limitless canvas of time and space, which many refer to as God.

Satisfaction doesn't come up on its own. One has to work with the 'elements of nature' to bring it upon oneself, actively. And then it's not easy to let go.

	Scientific	Popular	Philosophical
Space	A limitless, three-dimensional expanse in which celestial objects and events occur and have relative position and direction.	Space is everything in the universe beyond the top of the Earth's atmosphere.	For Arthur C. Clarke, if our universe were destroyed, space would be left behind. In that way, space is God since God is indestructible.
Time	Time can be considered the fourth dimension of reality, used to describe events in three-dimensional space. Time depicts the progression of events from the past to the present and into the future.	Time is a non-material substance which creates every moment in the material world. A period, either long or short, during which you do something, or something happens.	'Time', as per the ancient Hindu scriptures, is a wheel turning through vast cycles of creation and destruction. According to it, Time (Sanskrit *'kaal'*) is a manifestation of God. The past, the present and the future coexist in him simultaneously. One of the earliest recorded philosophies of time was expounded by the ancient Egyptians, considering the wasting of time as an abomination to the spirit.
Money	Money is a medium in which prices and values are expressed by both buyers and sellers. Money conceptually is portable, durable, uniform, divisible, acceptable, and in limited supply; hence valuable.	Money brings access. Access to things, resources and experiences which have an attached value, and which otherwise wouldn't be available freely.	Money brings about personal freedom. Plato and Aristotle suggested it as a non-object based on human action, a connector of exchange and a means without an end. The money you have, gives you freedom; the money you pursue enslaves you.
Satisfaction	The fulfilment or gratification of a desire, a need, or an appetite and the pleasure or contentment that is derived from such gratification. And if it is sustained… it leads to Life Satisfaction.	Satisfaction is the good feeling that you have when you have achieved something or when something you want to happen does happen.	Satisfaction is when you discover your purpose in life and therefore develop a favourable attitude towards one's life as a whole. Plato believed that a happy person is one who has principles and sticks to them. He or she uses and practices these principles in order to become a better person and a better member of society.

The big question then, is how are **Time, Space and Money** interacting with each other and playing out for each of us in the Universe to bring about and manifest the supreme goal of **Satisfaction** and lifelong contentment?

Thought Break

Before we proceed further to understand Time and Money, let's gather some insights through these enquiries:

- What is most important on your deathbed? In other words, what are you most likely to regret the lack of?

  Pick one.

  ☐ - Time

  ☐ - Money

- On a scale of 1-10, how serious are you to get what you want most? 10 being the most serious.

  1   2   3   4   5   6   7   8   9   10

- What should you 'control today' to 'get' what you want the most?

  Pick one.

  ☐ - Time

  ☐ - Money

If your answer to the last question is **Time**, here's a high-level view of how much control we exercise over the Time we have.

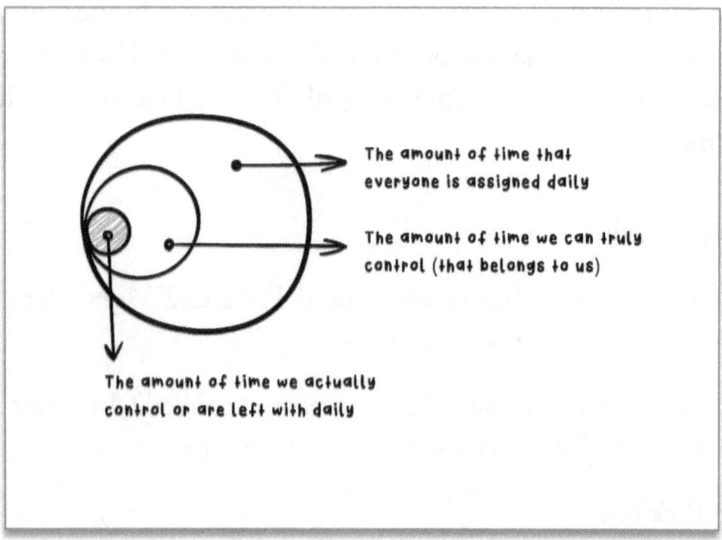

Pic 1: Circle of Control

Even if you answered **Money**, Time is where you will need to start anyway.

Look out for these themes in the next few chapters.

1. Time and money are in limited supply, hence valuable.
2. The natural tendency of money is also to get spent. However, we can still wield some control over it.
3. 'Time' comes in 'leaky packages' to us. It gets spent continuously. Once spent, it is spent; and one has to wait for the next package to arrive. And likewise, there are limited packages of time in one's life.
4. The only way to maximise the value of money is by judicious usage and good monetary habits; and the way to maximise the value of time is also by habits.
5. How can we make sense of what Plato said about 'principles' and stick to them?

Let's see what we mean by this in the next few chapters.

3. Time, Money, Expectations, Potential, Achievements

Life is a Balance of holding on and letting go.

'Time is Money' is perhaps the most cliched and overused phrase, yet the least understood and utilised approach in life.

Benjamin Franklin said that a few hundred years back, but even today, it is one of the smallest sentences that makes the greatest sense.

If we casually glance at the lives of Viraj, Romel, and Aneela, it is apparent that they all miss something or another. Something makes them fall short of that elusive feeling of being content, secure, and satisfied with their current beings and the path they are on.

Perhaps the lack of time, money (and resources), or perhaps both, leads to that nagging sense of incompleteness.

It seems:

Viraj: Has just enough money but not enough time.

Romel: Has enough money but no time and health

Aneela: Has no money and a feeling of no time and direction.

They seem to be riding a **W curve** through various stages in their lives. Time tends to get (W)asted or spent continuously.

This is fine if one is able to make (M)oney alongside riding the **M curve** and balancing the W, hand in hand.

In short, if your 'Time' (your own disposable amount of time) or 'Time at hand' graph is going **W**, then ideally your 'Money' (Earnings, access, and resource) graph should ride an **M**. That would give the ideal Time and Money balance.

Here are the hypothetical Time and Money graphs.

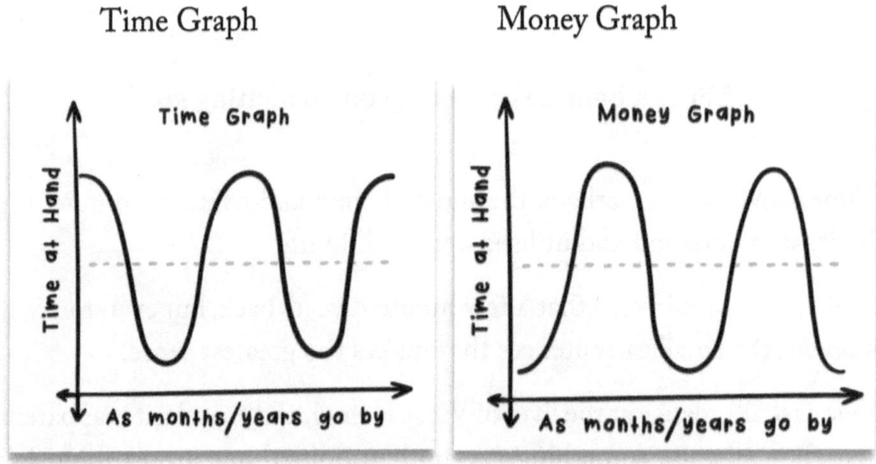

The Time and Money Balanced Graph: The Ideal Graph.

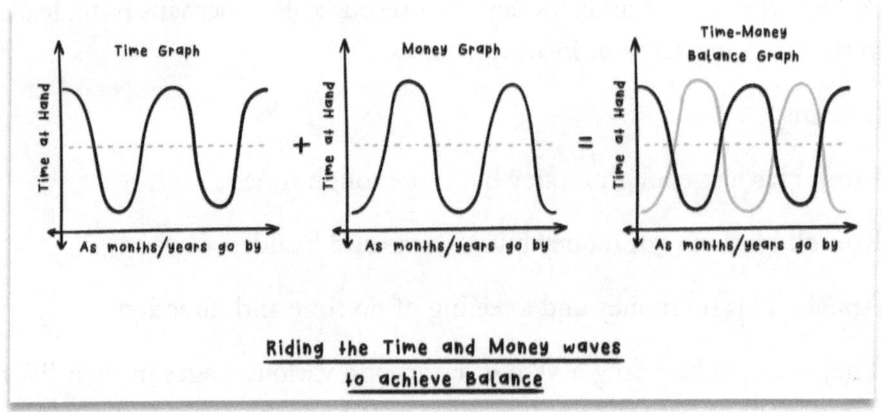

Pic 2: Time and Money Balance

The 'ideal graph' is what everyone should strive for. Why strive? Because it is **not** by default. The randomness of the Universe comes in the way.

The Random Universe

The natural tendency of everything in the Universe is **randomness**. Everything left on its own would either disintegrate, flow away, or transform into something else.

The most famous scientific equation in the world, Einstein's $E = mc^2$ says, Energy and Mass (matter) are interchangeable. They are different forms of the same thing and can be converted into one another (Mass-Energy equivalence or Law of Conservation of Mass-Energy).

In another way, it means that the total amount of mass and energy in the universe is constant.

Interestingly, ancient Hindu scriptures (Yajurved) documented these theories thousands of years ago. *Yatha Pinde, Tatha Brahmande; Yatha Brahmande, Tatha Pinde* – As is the individual, so is the universe and vice versa.

Even if modern-day scientists hadn't proved these by mathematical formulae, one could easily assume that such age-old wisdom must be logical and true.

So essentially, it brings us to the starting point that ALL forms of Matter and Energy follow the same rule. Time and money are no exceptions; neither is their influence on and interaction with the human body and soul.

In that case, how did the laws of the Universe also apply to the lives of Viraj, Romel, and Aneela in terms of their relationship with Time and Money?

Did they lack something, to begin with, or did they acquire that deficiency on their way?

Time and Money bear the same relationship as between Energy and Mass. Time is a form of Energy and Money is Mass (matter).

The timeless assumptions or maybe truths

Not only for our 'under the lens' trio (Viraj, Romel, Aneela), but certain assumptions, rules, and truths are playing out equally for all of us. Then how is it that each one of us charts a slightly different and sometimes entirely unique path for ourselves?

Let's begin by standardizing the assumptions.

1. **Total time available to us:** God (or Space) gave us all equal chances and accesses when we started our tenure on Earth. In terms of the fixed amount of TIME available daily to each of us, everyone is born rich. In fact, in a whole lifetime, 24 hours per day is substantial. It is about 2.5 billion seconds if someone lives for about 75 years.

   Let's take 8 hours out for the body to rest. We still get 16 hours fully awake and conscious, which is a huge 58000 seconds. In many ways, a single day in our lives gives us 58000 opportunities to think, decide, take resolve, initiate action, and so on.

   But even 16 core hours may not be enough for many, and they wish an Earth Day could have more hours. That's not going to happen, at least not in this lifetime. And if we are still insistent, we could try moving to some other planets with a longer day. Mercury, Venus, and Mars are the only other planets in our solar system you can set your foot on. They have terra firma (Firm terrain or land). However, none are habitable due to their unsuitable temperature and atmosphere!

   Earth is the best chance we've got. The only 'material' thing God could've given us is right here. A planet to call our home and 24 hours in each of our Bank accounts.

   In a lifetime of 75 years, all of us will be 'Time Billionaires', a term coined by Graham Duncan. That's quite rich!

2. **The true capacity of the brain:** Every brain is underutilised. But it depends on how we read this sentence. It's true, but not true at the same time.

   - The human brain is underutilised, and only 10% of it is used. This is a myth if we think of the brain only as a physical, functioning unit operating like a well-oiled engine. Physically, the brain is a gas-guzzling machine, constituting only 2% of the body weight but consuming more than 20-25% of the body's energy quota. In short, the brain cells are busy running our bodily functions (even during sleep) whether we realise it or not. And when we are consciously busy thinking, fighting, arguing, performing, or simply saving ourselves from adversities, the activity levels can go as high as 80-90%.

   - However, this statement about the 'Underutilised' brain could be a 'Truth' if we consider what most human beings do with the knowledge, information, and insights that the brain provides us with. Perhaps in that sense, the value that we can derive from our brain's processing in aspects of thinking, social interactions, learning, discipline, and habits is grossly underused. Human brain is capable of 'Thinking' and 'Directing' far more than we normally entrust it to do.

   - It is like having the world's best race car engine in the boot and the best driver on the wheels, yet all we do with that is take practice rounds on sanitised tracks. The machine never gets a chance to go full speed, and the driver never learns the whims of the car. Despite being fully loaded and functioning, the car never reaches its full potential.

3. **Our biggest asset:** Most of us give the least attention to our biggest asset and the most attention to a byproduct of it. TIME is the earliest and most tangible asset that we inherit when

we are born. Yet most of our efforts and energies focus on the byproduct, which is MONEY.

It is, in many ways, like putting the cart before the horse.

Money will follow if we take care of the time, spend, and invest it well. That's the rule of nature.

The later chapters will explain the dynamics of Time and Money and the factors that influence the relationship.

4. **Our true Potential:** Just like all of us have a finite package of time, we do come with a certain level of 'potential' that is inbuilt in us and, to some extent, gets shaped by the environment we grow up in.

   To begin with, let's assume a fixed potential that each of us possesses at birth. The best journey one could then ever take in their lifetime would be to reach that potential fully. At the end, finding the intersection point where our Achievements, Potential, and Expectations meet is a pursuit worth its effort and time. We will call it the **APE™** triangle.

Let us understand those better and use the concepts to navigate through the rest of the book.

1. APE™ Triangle diagram and brief
2. We learned about T-M. What about a TMS Balance (Time-Money-Satisfaction)?

The APE™ Triangle

Let us consider a set of three triangles which share a common centre.

A = Achievement

The innermost triangle is A (Achievement). Our collective successes, milestones, and accomplishments so far. Depending on our concrete achievements, this triangle can be represented as expanding or contracting in size around the common centre.

P = Potential

The middle triangle is P (Potential). To drive the point, we would consider an individual's potential as fixed. This triangle cannot change its size and is static. It assumes that all of us have a certain potential/capability, and it doesn't usually change that easily unless we put in additional effort by upskilling ourselves via training, exposure, and practice.

E = Expectation

This is the outermost triangle, E (Expectation). It is the collection of the bunch of desires, unfulfilled goals, and ambitions that we nurture as we go along our lives.

Baseline APE

This is how the triangles are aligned during most of our lives **until** we take control of our circumstances and decisions. This is the **Baseline APE Triangle.** This is where many of us usually are, even as we speak.

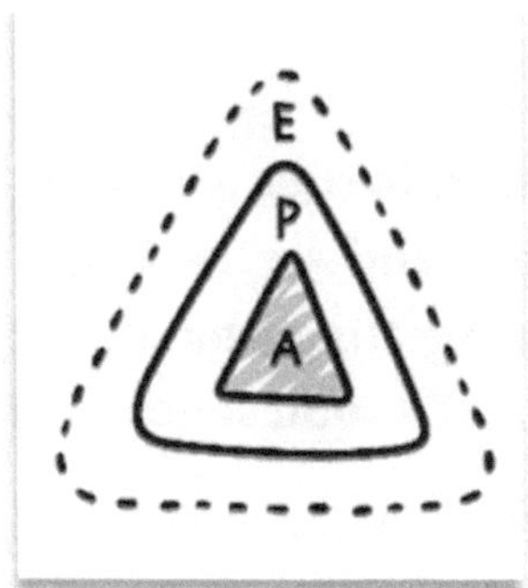

Pic 3: Baseline APE™ Triangle

While our Expectations are higher than our true potential, our achievements are also not at par with our potential. Notwithstanding any other aspects, this gap between our potential, achievements, and expectations is damaging and unsustainable. This gap could be one of our biggest hurdles to happiness and satisfaction.

On the other hand, there is the **Satisfied APE Triangle (the Solid APE).** This is what is the Ideal/Satisfied Triangle OR the solid APE **at the height of fulfilment** looks like. This is where our Potential, Expectations, and Achievements are completely aligned as if there was only one triangle, not three.

This is where there are no more unmet expectations, and we are fully satisfied and at ease with ourselves.

Pic 4: Solid APE™

A stage in life where you are in tune with yourself and generally happy with whatever you've got and are looking forward to. The simple reason is that you are now getting what you expect and are capable of. There is no disconnect. It's a solid state of contentment.

Would it be fair to say then that the entire journey is about how to move from **'Baseline to Satisfied'**? Theoretically, this could be a stepwise approach. In practical terms, we would walk the talk in chapter 7.

So, do we stop where our Achievements, Expectations, and Potential align?

One could perhaps tend to slow down, but achieving a fulfilled and content, comfortable state of mind doesn't mean complacency.

Instead, it should prompt you to think whether you want to 'expand your comfort zone' (**not 'move out'** of your comfort zone), expand your potential (take up a new challenge, exposure, or a pursuit); without creating unnecessary turmoil and getting trapped in new expectations which are beyond reasonable reach.

Even while we are expanding our comfort zone, keep the expectations in control (remember Gita, the cornerstone of Indian philosophy); but remain biased for action.

One of the oldest Egyptian thinkers, *Ptahhotep* (c. 2650–2600 BC), also mentions:

"Follow your desire as long as you live, and do not perform more than is ordered. Do not lessen the time of following your desire, for wasting time is an abomination to the spirit".

Ptahhotep means when he says, 'do not perform more than is ordered', that we should certainly chase our dreams and ambitions, but we should also know our true potential and boundaries and set our expectations accordingly. And once we have set our correct expectations, we just need to act and focus on it without wasting time.

Time Money Satisfaction (TMS) Triangle

In Geometry, it is interesting to know that a triangle, no matter its shape, would always have its internal angles in a way that the sum of the 3 angles will always be 180 deg.

For argument's sake, if we consider this 180 as a constant, then no matter what the shape of the triangle is, the eventual sum of its internal angles will always be 180.

Just like the law of thermodynamics, let's assume this 180 is constant and comes as a limited quota of the time, money, and satisfaction we would have in our lives.

The 3 sides of the triangle are then Time (T), Money (M), and Satisfaction (S).

Suppose we decide what our satisfaction level is and fix that as the Base of the Triangle. That leaves the T and M to move freely and assume any shape as long as the Base of the Triangle remains fixed to a certain length.

Our awareness and agreement with the BASE (Satisfaction) have to be stable and strong.

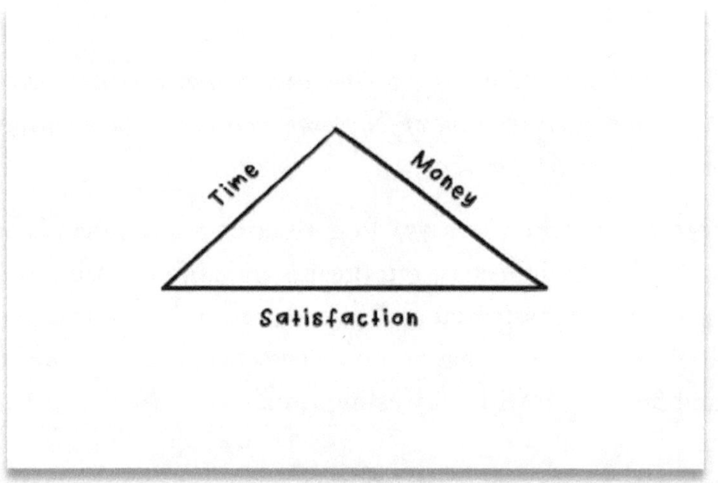

Pic 5: The perfect balance of Time, Money, and Satisfaction (Base should be Strong; Time and Money should be balanced without impacting the Satisfaction base).

More about it in Chapter 3.

The ideal situation is an Equilateral Triangle with T, M, and S perfectly symmetrical and balanced. We have the right amount of Time, Money, and Satisfaction in our lives.

However, based on our stage, we can vary our focus on the Time and Money aspects as long as we keep an eye on maintaining our satisfaction.

Typically:

1. T>M when one is starting up in his life/career. We have relatively more time at hand.
2. M>T when one is in midlife or career. We have relatively more money at hand.

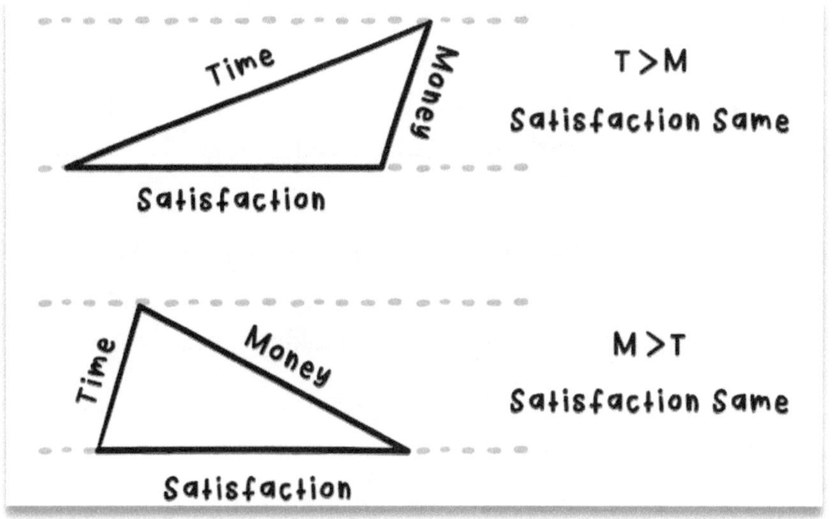

Pic 6: The TMS balance

Dilemma

It may seem like most people will have more money in their mid-life or mid-career phase, and they should be the happiest during that time. And therefore, happiness/contentment/satisfaction, etc., should be linked directly and proportionally to access to money, power, privilege, and so on. However, that is not the case, and in fact, most of the dilemma and existential crises that human beings encounter is during this phase of career and life.

If we do find a person who is rich and powerful and equally contended, one can be sure that money (and access) is just one of the reasons and NOT the only reason.

In fact, in all cases, what defines the chances of one being happy and contended is the APE.

In that sense, the entire journey is about aligning the APE triangles and not exactly about amassing the proverbial 'Money and muscle power'.

Money and time are only the means to the end (APE).

Bottomline: The journey towards a Solid APE is made smoother and more predictable when you control your TMS Triangle. Knowing where our satisfaction lies and gaining control over our TMS Triangle can exponentially increase our chances of being satisfied and remaining happy.

Since the APE and the TMS triangles are integral to the pursuit of happiness, we will discuss them more in chapters 6 and 7. And then, we will see how to use those in our decision-making processes.

But then let's come back to the same germinal question, what is more important, Money or Time?

The time comes in a leaky bucket. So, make that 'bucket list' fast.

The Mechanics of the Story

4. "Time: Money". The Omnipresent Currencies

The Equation and its Effect on Careers

Benjamin Franklin was one of the founding fathers of the USA, an accomplished publisher, author, scientist and inventor, and an astute politician and diplomat. Many of us may also not know his pseudonym, Richard Saunders.

Even he wondered and concluded about what was more important. Was he creating more money (or opportunities of earning) or creating (and saving) more time?

And he hypothesised while himself practising a certain routine. He certainly knew his 'Time' and was one of the richest men of his era.

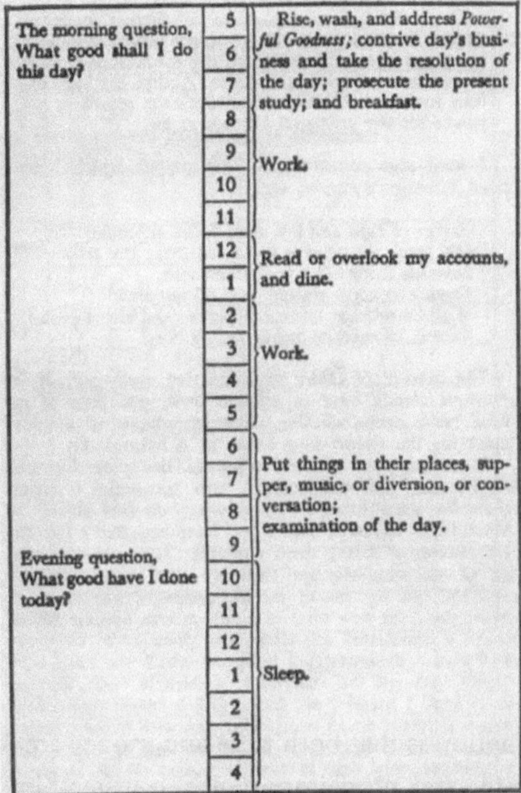

Pic 7: Benjamin Franklin's typical daily routine.

Knowing what he achieved in his lifetime, there is certainly merit in believing when he said, 'Time is Money'.

Let's deconstruct the perennial question; "Make Time or Make Money"?

Think about it; both seem important (of course!)

1. But are they both important at the same time and to the same extent?
2. At what life stage or phase of professional life is one more important/relevant than the other?

The idea of the Time (Effort): Money (Income/Resources) equation comes here. Probably a fresh look at the saying "Time is Money" is needed.

Assumption:

The basic assumption is that both time and money are "currencies" and are interchangeable and, more importantly, transferable.

Remember what Newton's law of thermodynamics says about the interchangeability of Energy and Matter. As per some philosophical beliefs, 'Time' is a form of Energy, and 'Money' is Matter (the root of the material world).

Let that sink in for a while.

How?

1. I can use my time (effort) on something or someone else… and in that process, I can gain or lose, or remain in a neutral position.
2. The same is true for money/resources. I can use my money/resources for something or someone else….and in that process, I can gain or lose, or remain neutral.

Time/Money relationship

One look at any life or career journey, and we realise 3 key things.

1. As we go deeper into our careers, the proportion of available 'Time' decreases i.e., the amount of disposable time available to us reduces.
2. The amount of 'income or resources' and capability of procuring material possessions increases relatively (and in most cases).
3. At different stages of our career and personal lives, the relative proportion of disposable time and disposable income have different values. At the beginning of our careers (where money is scarce), we need to spend time earning/buying money. And at later stages (where time is scarce), we need to spend money to earn/repurchase time. Remember, Time and Money are 'interchangeable currencies'.

In short, these 2 variables (Time and Money) can "buy" each other.

What would it be like if we plotted the 'Disposable Time Available' and the 'Income/Money/Resources accumulated' against the 'Number of Years spent in Employment'.

Disposable time available: The amount of time that is completely at your disposal and you have full control over it. This could be the time available to you after deducting the time you have committed to a job or a contract.

Income/Money/Resources accumulated: The amount of access, privileges, comforts, immunity, that you can procure by spending the money you already have. This is the money that you have full ownership of.

Let us look at a few life graphs to demonstrate the different ways of using our time and hence achieve different results.

Would the graphs give us a clue about what is happening with the 3 lives (Viraj, Aneela and Romel) we spoke about?

The Composed Viraj (The Safe, 'too safe' graph)

This is Viraj. The ever-cautious, risk-averse, always politically and socially correct being.

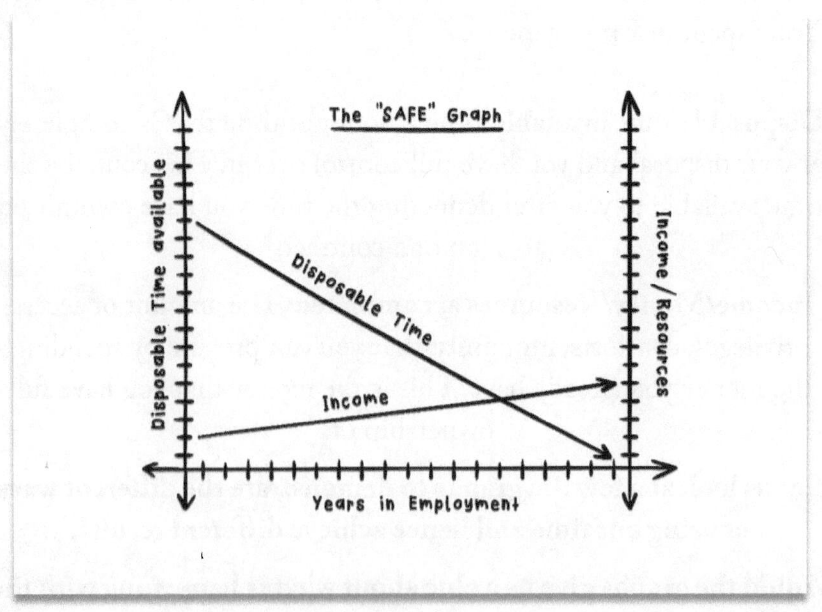

Pic 8: The Safe Graph

- He has been in steady employment, spending time and accumulating resources in proportion. Not too adventurous but safe and modest. The graph clearly depicts that perhaps Viraj has been 'too safe'.
- The free/disposable time available to him is reducing in proportion as he is investing time in his career and engaging in other personal/family/social commitments.
- His income/resources line could have been steeper.
- Although now, he has largely reconciled with his modest career, pangs of regret strike him occasionally. He does believe that, although late, he has a renewed desire to take some chances.

So, what's next for Viraj?

Perhaps Viraj should now look for opportunities to create long-lasting personal habits, invest Money, and make lifestyle changes that give him access to more Time (which is getting scarce for him).

Having access to more time may give him another chance to make money and create more resources for himself. If more money is not a priority at this stage, then at least he would get some more time to pursue other interests, keep spending quality time with his family, and plan for that dream international holiday well in advance.

Notes:

- **He certainly needs to break the linearity of his income.**
- **In other words, as days, and months and years go by, his time utilization should yield more money per unit of time spent. His time should become more valuable going forward.**

Do you know someone who is living through this kind of graph as we speak?

☐ - **Yes**

☐ - **No**

The Super Smart Romel (The 'Fast Track' graph)

Say 'Hi' to Romel. The confident, eloquent superstar, hobnobbing with CXOs and hounded by the media.

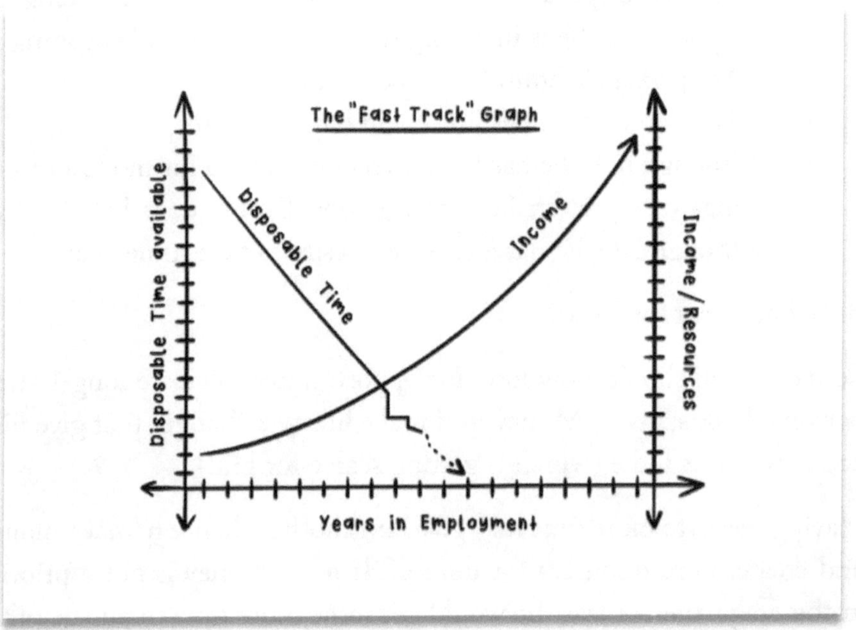

Pic 9: The Fast Track Graph

He has been a high-flying super-achiever, spending time extra-productively (and almost always investing his personal time too in that pursuit). He accumulated resources faster and many folds more than all his peers and seniors.

- Notice those dips in the Time curve (dips in disposable time) and peaks in the resources curve occurring simultaneously. More time he invests, for money he gets.
- As a result, the free/disposable time available to him is depleting at an alarmingly fast rate, as he continues to spend a very high proportion of his time in the career; while ignoring personal/social commitments.

- Lately, he has started questioning his choices and priorities about his health and life in general.
- These days, he says dryly, 'I must've lost more money on my surgeries and rehab than I ever did in the stock markets'.
- He has grown exponentially in monetary terms. The value of his time has always been high. He has been earning far more than the quantum of time he spent. Although he broke the Linearity of Income, there has been a rapid decline in his available/ disposable time.

So, what next for Romel?

Now that he is already feeling anxious about his health and wants to slow down, he should look for opportunities to invest some of his accumulated money in creating long-lasting habits and lifestyle changes, which could give him access to more Time (which is getting scarce for him) and strike the right work-life balance.

Notes:

- **He should now look at a prioritised list of things he needs to focus on. Wherever possible, he should spend money to buy time. And that time should be put into himself without any expectation of returns.**
- **That time should make him comfortable and let him regain his health, whether it is by taking longer breaks from work, holidaying or staying next to the office, or perhaps planning an early retirement and pursuing other interests directly under his control.**

This will also position him to create a renewed chance of recouping the joys of life and reinventing his zeal for an impactful yet balanced work life.

Do you know someone who is going through this dilemma as we speak?

☐ - **Yes**

☐ - **No**

The Mercurial Aneela (The 'Laggard' graph)

Meet Aneela. The intelligent, lively social creature, brightening up every gathering, perhaps holding the world record of having the maximum number of online friends.

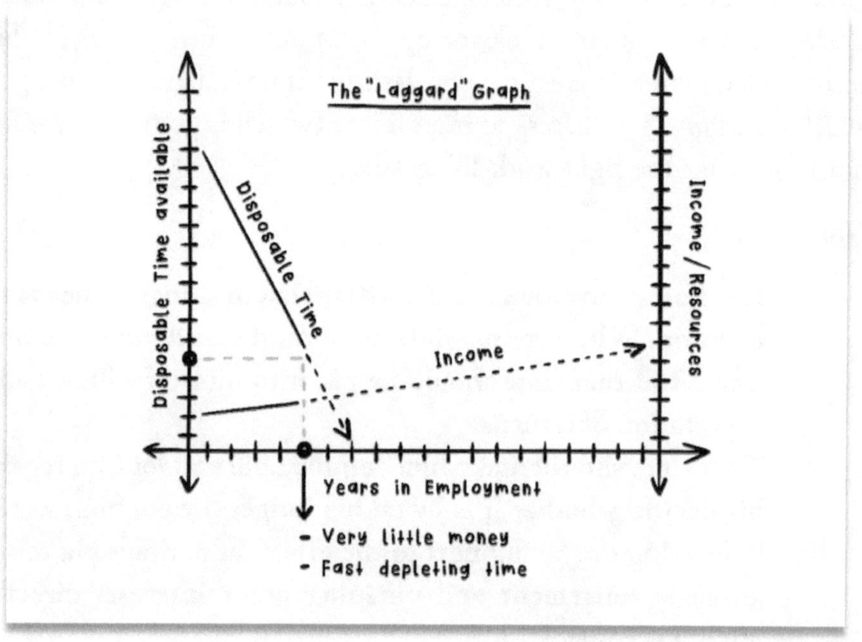

Pic 10: The Laggard Graph

In the beginning like everybody, Aneela too had lots of time at her disposal. But most of this time was either spent on entertainment or socializing. Basically, her own time being spent on others non-stop and purposelessly.

- As a result, the free/disposable time available to her was depleted fast, even before she realised it. By the time reality hit her, she saw that she had not converted enough of her time to create money/opportunities early on.
- Notice on the graph how little time she's left with and hasn't even properly started to make money.
- She would have very limited money/flexibility to get that spent time back. Not at least if she continued the same lifestyle.
- Constrained by the lack of money and time, all at once… she desperately needed either of these back in her kitty.

How should Aneela come out of this mess now?

- Without delay, she must make **drastic lifestyle and mindset changes** about the (monetary) value of time.
- Be cognizant of the fact that her "personal time", if not being used by her for any gainful pursuit, is lost forever, and someone else might be using it to create equivalent resources.
- She must use the **"Utility Filter"** (More about the Utility Filter in chapter 7 and Appendix).
- It essentially says:
    > 'If I spend some time doing something which is directly linked to generating money/resources/more time/or better health, then it is worth pursuing. Otherwise, it means someone else is using my time to get where I should be going/should have been'.

Thankfully, armed with this profound insight, she moved to a 'non-glamorous' profile in a smaller city in an equally non-pretentious company. Perhaps the best decision in her eventful life thus far.

Do you know someone who is on the verge of taking matters into his/ her own hands?

☐ - **Yes**

☐ - **No**

So, if Viraj, Romel, and Aneela all had something going wrong, is it even possible for someone to have the 'perfect' or at least a 'great' Time-Money graph?

The 'Balanced Fast Track' graph

Before we move into an example of a 'great' Time-Money graph, let's look back at Aneela's graph. Let's consider the lowest point for Aneela as the starting point of a brand-new curve. Full of hope and anticipation and brimming with choices.

And with that start, let's see how Aneela's journey looks like, fast-forward 15 years.

Phase 1 of Aneela's rebirth:

Recall how she had neither money nor time at the lowest point of her career and life. She was a desperate 'Laggard'.

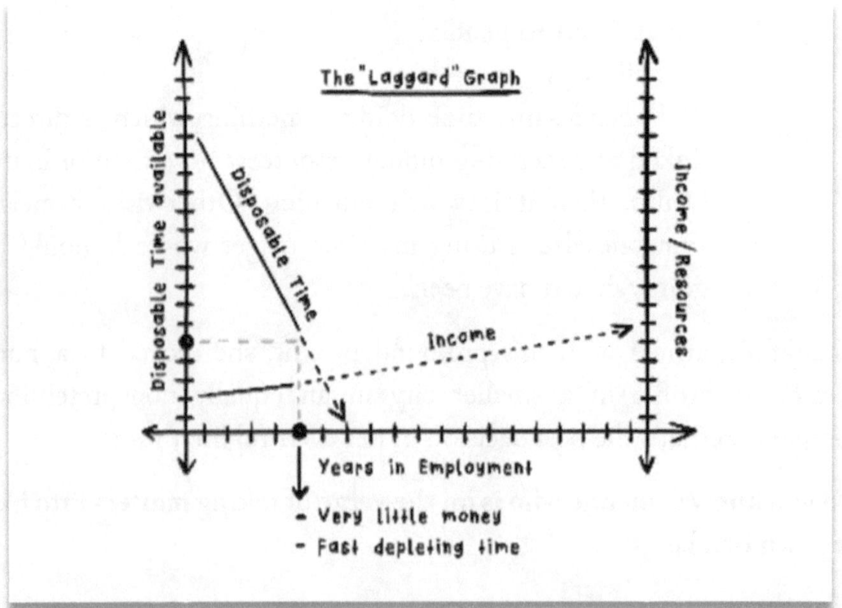

Therefore, for the first 2-3 years of her rebirth phase, Aneela put her head down and focused relentlessly on recovering the hours of disposable time back in her calendar. Her target in the 'Recovery phase' was to create at least 4-5 hours and keep complete control of that.

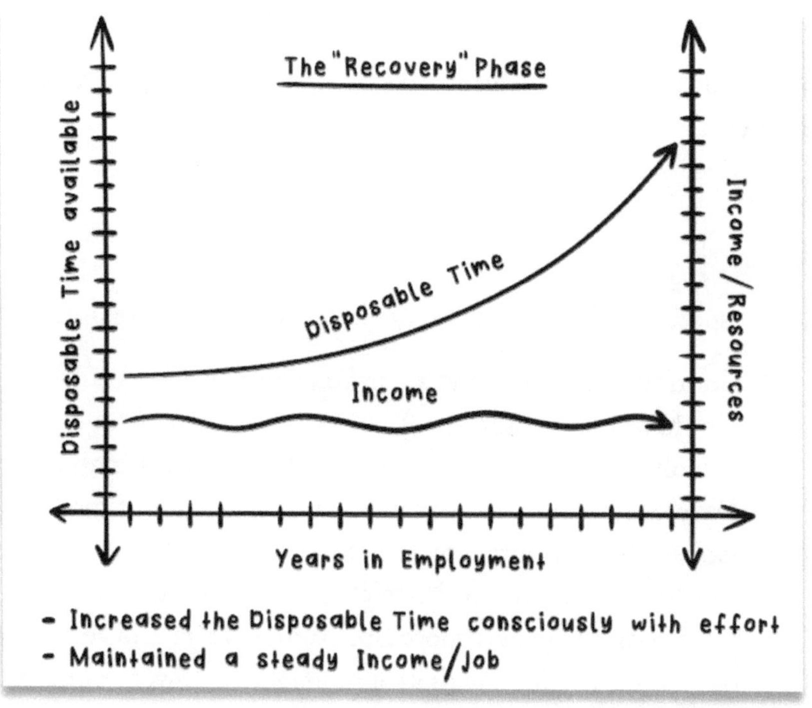

Pic 11: The Recovery Phase

She started by:

1. Shunning TV
2. Cutting down on social media and entertainment for 6 months
3. Journaling her daily observations and learning
4. Hiring a cook at home
5. Sleeping more, meditating
6. Getting herself a consistency coach

Phase 2 of Aneela's rebirth:

In 3 years, her 'disposable time' was back at the level when she started her professional career. She built some habits which allowed her to save at least 4 hours from her daily routine. She felt in control.

All she now needed was to sustain at that level and start including some of the best principles of the Time-Money conversion paradigm.

Do you know someone who would be interested in gaining control like Aneela?

☐ - **Yes**

☐ - **No**

What in specific did Aneela do to get back on track and maintain that?

- Continued to watch and spent time judiciously.
- Got herself a mentor.
- It took some very hard decisions to fight procrastination.
- Developed habits that encouraged investment of time to create money through her career, including, e.g., completing at least 1 online certificate course related to her profession.
- Gave proportionately more time to her career and took certain risks in opting for tough assignments which were more visible to management.
- In order to strike the right balance and not stress out, she continued to focus on her physical and mental health. She did it by practising yoga consistently for 30 minutes every day.

However, in a few years, she noticed that the free/disposable time available to her was again depleting as she continued to invest a substantial proportion of her time in her career goals. That's when her personal milestones were also vying for attention. She got married.

And then, her battle was about balancing her personal/social commitments and the thriving career she had created for herself.

Did Aneela finally make sense of all that? And was she able to strike the right balance finally, after having gone through a tumultuous start to her career, which had threatened everything at one point?

The Balanced Fast Track graph says it all.

Aneela started looking for opportunities to invest some of her accumulated money to give her access to more time (which was very scarce following a couple of promotions and having her first child). After striking the right work-life balance, it positioned her strongly in her career, as now she had time to focus on work and home both.

She was now trading in Time and Money currencies like an expert. She knew exactly when to buy what and at what price.

The interchangeability of these two universal currencies worked like magic.

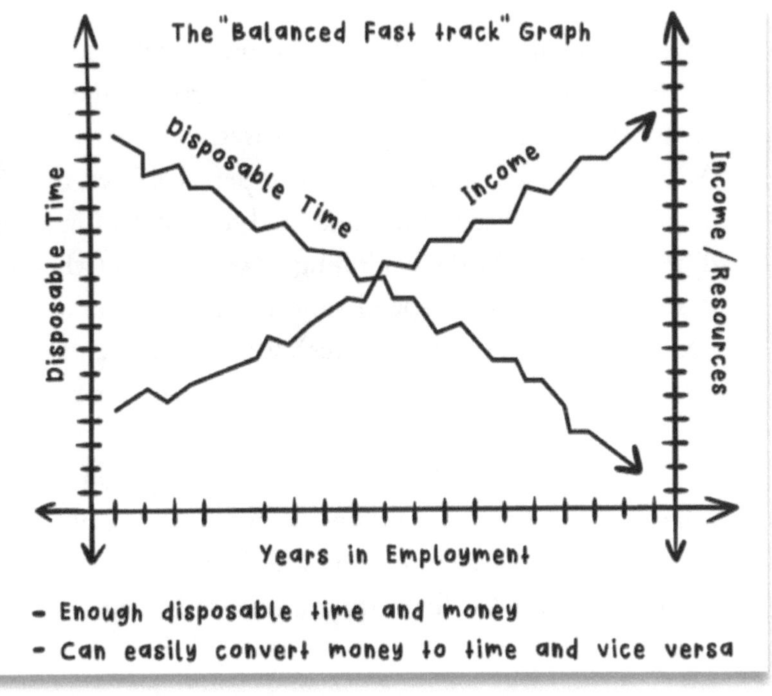

Pic 12: The Balanced Fast Track Graph

Her husband, who knew her from her school days, started calling her Karishma. The Indian word for miracles.

Yes, the same Karishma who started as Aneela and transformed herself into a miracle. The same Karishma who saw Viraj, Romel, and 'Aneela' from very close quarters and gave us invaluable insights into their lives and careers.

For our 4 characters, Viraj, Romel, and Aneela/Karishma, whatever happened, happened; but what were the underlying dynamics, habits, twists of time, and fate that led to the respective outcomes?

If those could be studied and codified, wouldn't it help millions of us?

Before we get there, let's summarise:

1. As we go deeper into our careers, the proportion of available "Time" decreases, i.e., the amount of disposable time available to us reduces.
2. Provided we make the right choices consistently and early on in our lives, the amount of "Income or resources" and capability of procuring material possessions increases.
3. At different stages of our career and personal lives, the relative proportion of disposable time and disposable income has different values. At the beginning of our careers (when money is scarce), we need to spend time for earning money. And at later stages (where time is scarce), we need to spend money to earn time. Remember, time and money are "interchangeable currencies".
4. In short, these 2 variables (Time and Money) can "Buy" each other... and it depends on how we use our disposable time, to buy more time OR more money OR better health (Physical, Mental, Family), Or for getting a new, satisfying hobby/social cause.

As a thumb rule, though, creating more productive time within those 24 hours seems to be the logical first step towards

greater resources, happiness, and satisfaction. Money is just an intermediary. What is important are the choices we make consistently and for a steady period.

*　　　　　*

Karishma didn't realise when she had dozed off, with the almost empty cup of mint tea still on her lap. After waking up from a welcome power nap, she remembered the deadline to submit her presentation to the Ministry of Education. Five of her students whom she sponsors in a social welfare NGO broke into the top 30 rank holders of the National School Board examinations. And they will all be felicitated by the President of the country a week later.

Karishma would also be there at the function to relish that high point in her life.

This high point would be the culmination of a roller coaster ride. From a life of privilege to frittering away everything, regaining much of it, and then pursuing a far more meaningful life.

The rest of our book is to help deconstruct the remarkable journey Aneela took to transform into a miracle…Karishma.

And if one thing is common between the lives of Aneela and Karishma, that is their changing relationship with time and…

Let's take a guess or find out on the next pages.

Time is more valuable than money. You can get more money, but you cannot get more time.

Time is forever depleting. Money is not.

If you stay still/do nothing for 1 hour, your bank balance may not reduce; but 60 minutes are gone.

So, prioritise time.

PART C

The Journey Ahead

Pit Stop 1

What do we know so far?

1. 'Time' is perhaps the most important tangible as well as intangible asset one has in one lifetime. Everything else derives from it.
2. Where do we stand in our Time-Money equation?
3. We all need to know where we stand on our APE graph.

Let's take an example from one of our own characters, **Aneela**:

1. Her T-M equation shows a severe shortage of disposable time.
2. She has already spent/wasted a chunk of her time on non-productive pursuits.
3. There is almost zero ROI (Return on Investment) for the time she has already spent.
4. Now that she needs some money to buy back her time, that's fallen inadequate.

What would we do if it was not Aneela but one of us?

1. Analyse the life so far with the help of your APE graph. Refer to the section on APE triangles in Chapter 3.
   1. Honestly assess your potential (for a certain target) and how much you have achieved.
   2. Look at your Expectations. Are we expecting more than our potential?
   3. In any case, work towards closing the gap between your A (Achievement) and P (Potential) and keep it that way. How?
2. First, agree on what stops you from "Achieving your full potential" and what is deficient; time, money, or both.
3. Analyse the daily decisions or choices you make.
   1. Are those choices 'Roadblocks' or 'Enablers' towards your achievements?

2. Are those choices contributing towards your deficiencies in time or money? E.g., quick fixes and easy choices/habits robbing you of your disposable time.

4. Agree on a **Goal** or Action to remove the roadblocks. Let's say carving out 2 hours from your day and investing in yourself towards working on that Goal/Action.

   1. The goal should be such that, if met, it should bring your Achievements closer to your Potential. (APE graph)
   2. Remember, this time, the approach towards the goal should differ from your earlier attempts.
   3. You need to understand and build a relationship with Choices, Decisions, Habits, Motivation, and Willpower. But the approach towards these elements must first be understood for sustained results and desired outcomes. In short, for achieving that 'goal'.

In the next couple of chapters, let's embark on this journey of self-discovery (of Aneela becoming Karishma), backed by Science and Behavioural Psychology, themes of Performance Management, Habit Formation, Prioritisation, and Consistency.

All in all, the next pages would simplify our pursuit and focus on the **minimum** that can be done to start off and see positive outcomes for every second we put into our days.

Big Tip:

What do we need more of? Time or Money?

We need to find out what we lack and then dip our hands in the other pool.

If both are empty, then take a hard look at the choices and the places you are spending your time and money.

5. The Choices (We Make) and The Results (We Get)

Life is an outcome of the millions and billions of choices we make.

At any moment in time, we are dealing with choices. Choices that are completely in our hands and which only we can make. And these choices almost always decide what will happen in the next moment or millions of moments later.

But of course, there are many other pre-programmed outcomes too which we do not have much control over.

Whether our heart beats or not, whether we continue to breathe in our sleep, whether our eyes blink 15000 times or more during the day. All of these are pretty out of our control. And neither are the mind-boggling questions around the future of Earth and humanity or, for that matter, the Solar System, and the Universe. We can only theorise about these. Can we accurately control or predict the outcomes? Perhaps not.

In a parallel world, we may still have some mechanism to control the outcomes, whether it be the human body or the elements of nature. However, it might come at a huge, unimaginable effort.

Remember the Circle of control diagram:

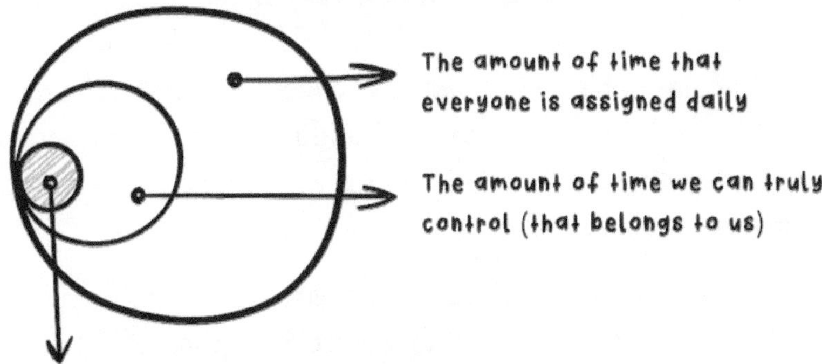

Therefore, let's stick to our choices for outcomes that we can control in our worldly realm and within the capacity of our individual selves.

Given 2 choices, which one will you pick from the below? Assume it's cold and windy outside.

- Switch on the 12-episode, super popular Netflix series and order a pizza
- Put on your shoes and windcheater and step out for a 20-minute jog

Most, if not all, will choose the 1st option. Why?

Before we start blaming human laziness and the need for comfort, our usual tendency to choose the easy path, etc., let's understand that this propensity to choose the easy option is not only natural but also universal. It transcends not only species but even inanimate objects. It's true for gravity and the laws of electricity, fluids, energy, and whatnot.

A bolt of electricity would flow through a wire with the least resistance. Water would flow from top to bottom; a hot cup of tea, on its own, would lose energy and become cold. These are the easy choices that Humans and the Universe find for themselves naturally.

Taking an easy path is not only a very human tendency but also natural and universal.

For anything else to happen, it would need external assistance. It would need additional effort. It would need additional time, energy, money, focus, commitment, diligence, discipline, and everything which means going against the natural choice.

In other words, the natural choice is the easiest and least cumbersome, whereas if one goes against a natural course, it requires effort.

Therefore, you would have to provide additional energy/effort to make that cup of tea hot again.

Hence, I would simply switch on Netflix and sink into my couch unless there is a dire need.

The Choice-Life Equation

Everything in nature has a purpose. If something has no utility, it perishes. The fact that something exists means that it has some value. And if it has some value, it wouldn't be easy to acquire and maintain.

If difficult choices had no takers, why would they even be there? Why would the mind even think about going for a jog on a cold, windy evening?

Why would we even think of moving water against the gravity?

These choices are difficult, quite difficult. But they exist because they are valuable, and they have the potential to change things in astonishing ways. These difficult choices that only a select band of humans took over millions of years have made Homo sapiens the dominant species in the natural world.

And within that ecosystem of modern human society, several bands of humans have done more meaningful work for themselves and society at large. They have made their own life, and the lives of millions, EASY, with their own 'difficult' choices.

And then millions of others took the easy choices and let their destinies flow naturally. The outcomes were completely up to the whims of the elements of nature and circumstances. One can't complain about that. It was YOUR choice to let it go the natural way.

And if, despite making the easy choices, your life turned out the way you imagined it to be, you could give the credit to 'Luck' and hope that your luck continues every time you relinquish control of your life to easy choices. But 'Hope' alone is never a good strategy.

Time and again, throughout human history, Easy choices have led to difficult lives; and Difficult choices have created some of the best moments and monuments on Earth and resulted in a relatively easy life for the ones who paid attention.

Here is a personal example that I won't forget.

I started typing out the manuscript of this book in offline mode on my personal computer. The plan was always to put it up in the cloud drive soon and continue to write. Then I changed my computer but continued to write in offline mode. Five months into the manuscript of the book, I was still taking it 'easy' and procrastinating. In the 7th month, with 90% of the book complete with all the data, pictures, and references, my laptop crashed.

It was nothing less than a disaster.

The chances of data recovery were minimal. I realised what a 'difficult' situation I had landed myself in due to my 'easy' choices.

The entire spectrum of Easy choices→Difficult Life; Difficult choices→Easy Life, played out like a movie in front of me.

Nightmarish as it was, it took me 6 additional months to recover and rewrite the lost portions.

Indeed, it's a life lesson.

Vestigial organs: Use them or lose them

Vestigial organs are those that today merely exist in the human body as remnants of an evolutionary past. They were useful a few thousand generations back, though.

The nictitating membrane in the eyes, the appendix, and the coccygeal bone were all serving some purpose in the human body as long as there was relevance. Those turned into some useless lump of tissues once the body stopped using them.

The same is true for Time and Money. Once you stop using your Time and Money judiciously, you might lose them forever.

Similarly, 'Difficult choices'. If difficult choices had no takers and no use, then why would they even exist in the universe?

Easy choices→Difficult Life; Difficult choices→Easy Life

(ECDL, DCEL)

But how do we identify something as an Easy Choice or a Difficult Choice?

Isn't something that I find easy, immensely difficult for someone else and vice versa?

Let's see the examples below.

Scenario: Putting on your shoes and going for a 20-minute jog on a cold evening.

It might be the most difficult decision for Jim, who's never really taken fitness seriously but now is mandated to lose weight. The other option he has is to perhaps take a light stroll in the garden for 5 mins, justifying it by hoping it would have the same benefits as the jog.

Yet, if Jim takes the above option of a 20-minute jog, it will certainly qualify as a 'Difficult' decision.

On the other hand, Ron, a fit, athletic person, who runs every day, and is preparing for a full marathon in 3 weeks, has 2 options.

- Going for that jog for 20 minutes, OR
- Spending an hour in the gym doing weights and then running for an hour on a sloppy terrain.

If Ron also chooses the 1st option, he wouldn't do justice to his choices. That is far too 'easy' for his baseline. He must go for a more rigorous practice routine to clock a decent time in his month-end full marathon.

Therefore, given a list of choices, we need to see which is the more difficult choice in relative terms and then decide consciously about the choice and our decision to take it.

Jim and Ron must agree and accept the outcomes of their respective choices. Even if both decide to take that 20-minute jog, the outcomes as per their expectations might completely vary.

It's anybody's guess who would be happier.

Let's recap.

How do you identify an easy choice?

Out of several options, the one that seems most comfortable and safe.

Which doesn't require us to challenge our physical or mental limits. Which we secretly justify as being the right thing to do, remaining in our comfort zone.

Easy choices are the ones we see most people make around us; hence, we are conditioned to think of those as the right choices. Easy choices are routine, and in the long run, boring. They keep us where we are and force us to let go of our control of time, money, and destiny.

Easy choices simply consume.

How do you identify a difficult choice?

Given several options, the ones that stretch you, that you wouldn't normally take, that you would be proud of if you take up and finish.

Difficult choices are the ones that most people would shy away from and will have justification against. Difficult choices help us grow. They take us places. Difficult choices produce new avenues, possibilities, and things.

BIG QUESTION:

Is it the easiest thing I am picking up from all the options?

Does it need me to be more disciplined?

How much is too much?

The above concept of **ECDL and DCEL** may sound simplistic.

If we assume that 'one' easy choice once in a while would create a Difficult life for you; that's not true. On the contrary, 'one' difficult choice taken once in a blue moon won't guarantee an Easy life.

When these easy or difficult choices are made 'consistently' over an extended period (over weeks, months, and years), they manifest their effects. Good or bad.

In other words, when those choices are made consistently and habitually, they become habits.

Habits

This manifestation of choices into a good or bad outcome is almost always due to what we call 'habits'.

'**Habit** is one of the most important predictors of a good or bad outcome'. Mark these words as you'll face them many times over.

Let's define habit.

Habits are those frequent and customary actions/behaviours that do not require much conscious effort and can take place automatically in settings that provide a consistent cue/trigger.

In simple terms, habits run on autopilot after they get firmly established in our subconscious and daily routine.

The 'Candid' list

Take a moment to list your habits (good and bad), from the basic 'washup and brushing' rituals of the morning, to fastening the seat belt while driving, to the obligatory swiping the screen of your smartphone every 2 minutes. Also, add habits that you had earlier but have given up on now.

1. ____

2. ____

3. ____

4. ____

5. ____

Your relationship with these habits might leave you better off, proud, or even guilty sometimes. They might either be simple basic daily habits or might be habits that are turning you into a more, or even less efficient and happy, healthy human being.

Whatever it is, habits GUARANTEE outcomes. Whatever you do today is an outcome of your habits.

There are only two types of people. The ones who would eat the tastiest dish first; the others who would save it for the last.

The Mechanics and Drivers of Habit Formation

So, if habits are so interlinked with outcomes, how are they related to the numerous daily choices throughout our lives?

Where is the tipping point when our choices and actions become habits and start delivering the Good and the Bad?

Habits can be spontaneous and get acquired unintended. For example, if you brush your teeth every day, it is certain that you picked up that habit when you were a kid assisted by the adults around. Though it was easy, there was perhaps no choice involved.

However, habits resulting from deliberate choices require effort and thinking. It doesn't matter whether the choice is easy or difficult. Even thinking about a choice is a deliberate act and requires effort (hence the term deliberation).

e.g.,

1. It might be a difficult choice to start a daily exercise schedule lasting 60 days.
2. However, deciding against continuing that exercise streak after a week might be easy, but it would still require a deliberate choice.

In both cases, you will form a habit. In the first case, you will end up exercising every day by default. In the second instance, you will be in the habit of finding excuses to not exercise. The choice is yours.

'Choice is the mother of habits'

Of course, the amount of effort needed to make a difficult choice is always high, and vice versa.

And when choices are made consistently and on autopilot, we call them habits.

Habits don't qualify themselves as good or bad. We as humans call out whether a habit is good or bad. As in whether the habit is an outcome of an easy or difficult choice.

e.g., Going for a light jog every morning without fail or consciously forcing oneself, could be a good habit. But it's definitely not an 'easy' choice until it becomes a habit.

Similarly, habits like reading or writing, going to bed early, digital detox, and moderation are all the outcomes of difficult, tough decisions. It takes time to acquire such desirable habits to be part of one's life.

On the other hand, habits like drinking soda 5 times a day are easy choices and can become a habit before you know it. How about watching a TV series non-stop?

So, why are bad habits so attractive and all around us, and good habits are so difficult to form?

Look back and see the kind of choices that drive habit formation. Review the answers you gave to the Candid list earlier in the chapter.

Which of those habits is an outcome of the easiest of choices?

How do you feel about them today?

Habits don't form in isolation. Either they are in response to some subconscious desire, a means to achieve a conscious goal, or plain and simple instant gratification. And as we saw earlier too, habits always lead to outcomes.

'Bad habits' form easily because they are rooted in easy choices, instant gratification, and sometimes circumstances. And more philosophically, due to the inherent nature of humans and the Universe to let things happen easily, spontaneously, and naturally. (Refer to the first section in this chapter)

It could be due to how we were raised or the surroundings. Those factors, one could say, are out of our control for the most part until we decide to change the course consciously and with effort.

However, when we make easy choices voluntarily, those are simply because we are following the natural tendency of life, the path of least resistance, the easy way.

But 'Why' do we opt for easy choices when we know that those may not be the best choices in the long run?

Because those easy choices require the least amount of energy and effort, so, there is comfort in easy choices, and 'Comfort is Addictive'. And addiction leads to consistently seeking that comfort. This vicious cycle definitely leads to specific BAD habits.

In short, every easy action or choice we make consistently/repeatedly might take us towards a bad habit.

The 'Good News' is one factor that is common to both Good and Bad habits. And that is CONSISTENCY. More about that a little later.

The Journey from Goal to Choice to Habit to Outcome

In the Pit Stop 1 chapter, we saw how important it is to do a gap analysis of our achievements and expectations through the APE graph. And to reduce that gap, we need to identify one or two **goals**.

Goals that would add something valuable and/or eliminate something useless/toxic from our lives.

To achieve those goals over a period, we need to make some difficult **choices** and decide to stick to the choices for as long as they need to become habits. Even the actions taken towards breaking/eliminating a bad habit can be termed a good **habit**.

But that's where the cookie crumbles. That's where the **outcome** eludes us.

What decides that we are able to stick to a difficult choice and turn it into a good habit? Many of us would not be able to complete even one cycle of choice to habits and would have to start again on the same journey without addressing the root cause of our disruption.

So, what will decide whether we will be able to carry on that difficult choice for 'N' days* without giving up?

Is it Willpower, Motivation, Self-Control, or Commitment to your goal?

---

* More about the ideal 'N' days in a later section.

The million-dollar question:

Is willpower really the only thing?

Is willpower (or Self-control, Motivation, Commitment) the only thing needed for 'Good' habit formation and Bad habit elimination?

It is nowhere but in the pursuit of 'good' habits that we associate willpower with.

It's counterintuitive, though.

If something is a good habit and will be beneficial in the mid to long term, why would we even need the additional support of willpower? The habit should ideally form easily.

But that's not the case. As we saw earlier, good habits are like long-term investments; they need time, thinking, and more importantly, effort to sustain a difficult choice.

So how important is willpower (or for that matter, 'motivation') in this equation?

In a unique study published in 2020, in *Front. Psychol,* titled *'How to Form Good Habits? A Longitudinal Field Study on the Role of Self-Control in Habit Formation*, it was the initial premise and quite logical that self-control, willpower, and motivation have a huge and deciding role to play in successful habit formation and perhaps in the attainment of goals.

However, the researchers found that Willpower, Self-control, and Motivation are only as much important as any other factors, if not less.

If you have willpower, fine, but that may not be enough to pull you through the entire duration until the habit is formed.

On the other hand, motivation is when your entire psychosomatic system (Mind and Body at the cellular level) is hyper-energised, and your adrenaline and motivation hormones are at their peak. You are ready to seize the moment and so on. All this is very dramatic. But it also means that the heightened and persistent attention only lasts for days and perhaps a few weeks. It comes in spikes and with a steep price tag.

Motivation, willpower, or self-control all require heavy-duty maintenance to sustain. And as someone said, rather unpopularly, 'Willpower and Motivation are overrated'.

But it's not easy to be convinced. What's wrong with Motivation, Willpower, and similar brute forces?

Nothing wrong, but there is a risk when the entire burden of habit formation lies only on the shoulders of willpower/motivation. When your motivation and willpower waver, so do your chances of habit formation and eventual goal attainment.

So, when motivation and willpower start fading away, what works best and will keep you afloat in your habit formation journey?

Although the study (2020, *Front. Psychol)* didn't look deeper into the role of self-control in avoiding distractions or temptations, it sounds reasonable that once you have started your habit journey, if at all you want to bring in motivation, do that in avoiding any temptations and easy choices on the path. Just keep focusing on continuity and persistence.

Consistency, Consistency, Consistency

Let's agree that we are on a long journey of habit formation and goal attainment, not a momentary motivation trip.

Although motivation is that intense bout of purpose and willingness to act, it wavers like the crest and trough of a wave. It is INCONSISTENT. And inconsistency is an enemy of habit formation.

Motivation, of course, is a great way to get started in anything. But once the start is made, it's a matter of time before the motivational level wanes again.

In that case, the best way to sustain this momentum would be to find a small, repeatable piece of action that you can commit to every day. An action that is PAD (Practical and Doable) and can be performed every day with minimal resistance. Every day until it becomes a habit.

Let's realise that when it comes to habit formation, **Consistency > Motivation**. Consistency might be mundane, but it delivers outcomes.

Motivation shows you the trailer, but consistency presents the whole movie to you.

Motivation is what you get when you strike a matchstick. It helps you light a candle before withering away. That candle is the consistent source of light you want, and you get.

Pic 13: The Consistent Candle

In your life, you need both, but you need the candle more. The candle is less dramatic but more consistent. Just as the candle delivers light, consistency delivers the outcome.

Similarly, you don't burst a loud cracker when you need warmth. You simply light a fireplace. The smoldering coal is less dramatic but serves the intended purpose for a long time.

What's your Trick, the Candle or the Matchstick?

It shouldn't be difficult to figure out.

M for Matchstick and so is Motivation.
C for Candle and so is Consistency.

Why is consistency so potent?

Consistency sneaks up upon you. It acts while you barely notice. Consistency is silent and less dramatic, but it packs a punch when it does. Depending on what we are consistent in, the end result could be either good or bad.

Couple of years back, my 80-year-old father bumped his head against a cupboard. Life was normal for about 6 months until we found him losing speech, memory, and control over his voluntary muscles. What seemed like a paralytic attack turned out to be a case of a very small capillary leak in his skull due to that minor bump. The blood leak had been so small that it took months to start spreading and turn into a massive gelatinous blob in the brain. The brain was crushed in half and lost most of its capacity.

It took a team of 3 neurosurgeons to clean that clot and plug the leak.

A microscopic leak, barely noticeable and ignored, consistently grew, and almost killed my father.

Did we hear Consistency again in the above sentence? Yes.

Consistency delivers outcomes

Consider the statements below.

1. As an ex-Navy Seal, David Goggins said, 'There is no better way to grow as a person than to do everyday something you hate'. By hate, he perhaps meant something which is a difficult choice.
2. If you want to be good at something (good at being even bad), the only way is to consistently do that 'something'. A bit every day…

For a while, think about the words from the above phrases, **grow, every day, difficult, choice, consistently.**

Here's another personal example. I remind myself of this every few days. And that helps me stay on track for some of the newer habits I am trying to form or give up some other habits which have outlived their utility.

5 years back, when my doctor told me to inculcate a habit of cardio exercises, I did everything from joining a gym to getting a treadmill at home to start running, a bicycle, and a personal trainer. The premise was that it would help me achieve the overall goal of losing about 6-7 kgs in a few months.

On good days I would clock almost 15-20 km of running and cycling. For some reason or other most of these routines/regimes would only last max for 5-7 days before I restarted.

At the end of one year of trying everything, getting motivated to do one thing over the other, I must've run about 250 km, bicycled around 500 km, and run 3-4 marathons (20 km each). Big numbers, right?

But something still wasn't right. I didn't feel I was in control of those activities. Those would be at the mercy of my mood, my office schedule, and my whims, and on top of that the tasks were daunting. Running and cycling for 15 km daily is not easy, and I wouldn't be motivated every day to do that. And there were days when I didn't run at all. I was regular, perhaps 4 out of 10 days. I was just not able to remain consistent. Moreover, I hadn't lost much weight that could be attributed to my running routine alone.

Was the target itself robbing me of my consistency and achievement of my overall goal?

Over the next 25-30 days of realising that I needed a change of tact, I reduced the daily target to 3 km, straight from 15 km to 3 km. And I had a self-talk about committing to this reduced and 'PAD' (Practical and Doable) target.

Though the target was reduced, my consistency in meeting that daily target shot up to 9 out of 10 days. After a few weeks, it felt easy. It indeed felt easy enough to increase my target to 5 km and eventually 7 km daily.

At the end of the year, I was more proud of this reduced yet consistent run, than I was of running those marathons and churning 20 km on some days.

With a 7 km daily routine for a year, I had covered a distance of almost Mumbai to Delhi and back. Now that is what I call a grand score. My 'once in a while' motivated, high visibility, glorious medal-flashing marathons could never do that.

When I look back and if we transpose this example to the various concepts we discussed earlier, the recurring theme turns out to be:

Choice and **Commitment to Consistency**.

These 3 C's, if supported by a little bit of D (Discipline), E (Effort), F (Frequency), and G (Grit), can give us H (Habit).

$$3C+D+E+F+G=H$$

3 C = Choice and Commitment to Consistency

D = Discipline (The difficult choices)

E = Effort (Acting even when you don't feel like it)

F = Frequency (Regularity)

G = Grit (Not giving up easily)

H = Habit (Effortless Autopilot)

One just has to commit to remain consistent. The rest will fall in place. This is your real CTC, (Commitment to Consistency)

Pic 14: Choose consistency over motivation

What is more important? Habit Formation or Goal Formation? And where do you start?

Spend 5 minutes and refresh Chapter 3 (APE™ graph and Pit stop 1)

After you've done your APE analysis, found the key gaps, and understood your choice patterns, you would identify a goal (A big, positive outcome). More about Goal formation in Chapter 7.

But that goal wouldn't simply stand up and say hello to you and meet itself while you watch over it.

You have to, in fact, break the goal down and PAD it up with small actions and outcomes. Each outcome would come together and take shape to start looking like the big outcome you are moving towards.

And what will deliver an 'outcome'?

A habit.

A consistent good habit is founded on a couple of difficult choices and is nourished by CTC (Commitment to Consistency) and some monitoring (and course correction).

Why should you believe the above statements?

In a study with volunteers wanting to lose weight, the researchers randomly assigned them to 2 groups. The 'Control group' was given a weight loss target and then left on their own.

The other (Test group) was similarly given the same target but also a few interventions like dietary and activity tips that needed to be repeated daily.

Both groups were asked to report back after 8 months.

The results were interesting but certainly not surprising.

The control group, which was left to lose weight on its own, didn't show much progress.

On the contrary, the test group that received the intervention reported back not only a significant average weight reduction but also evidence of habit formation. The test group members started showing results as early as 2 months as they consistently followed their daily routine.

As time progressed, and the members saw initial positive results, they repeated those small, sometimes difficult activities until they became daily habits and no longer required additional effort. In fact, members reported that they felt 'odd' if they missed the routine on a particular day.

Starting from day 1, the test group was on a habit formation journey which gave results, and by 8 months, the habits were firmly ingrained. Those habits became their 'second nature'. This test group had 'mastered their habits'.

But the control group that was not monitored or where interventions were not done relied solely on their daily flow and occasional motivation and awareness. It didn't get the advantage of consistency and repetition of actions because there was no monitoring or alarm system. The actions performed by this group didn't reach a critical tipping point where 'habit automaticity' could set in.

Without automaticity, you are not even aware of a habit. And sadly, it all leads to an unmet goal (in this case, weight loss).

In short, the goal will remain elusive until a strong habit is formed. Therefore, **Goal formation is important, but Habit formation is critical.**

Habit Formation > Goal Formation

Master your habits

Good habits are not 'Forced'. They are 'Formed'.

And when they are formed and ingrained, they can make way for other adjacent habits, which make the attainment of goals easier and faster.

e.g., Once you become habituated to clocking around 10000 steps every day, you would consciously want to eat relatively healthier lest you lose the advantage of your 10K walks. That, in turn, might make your sleep routine better in the long run.

And when you are on the journey of mastering a habit, focus on 'What' but more on 'How'.

What = Goal, and How = Habit. Without a 'How', the 'What' will remain a dream.

In short, mastering your habits can guarantee goal attainment. Although the word Mastering sounds a bit daunting, it is not. Here's some relief.

This is how it looks like when you've mastered your habits.

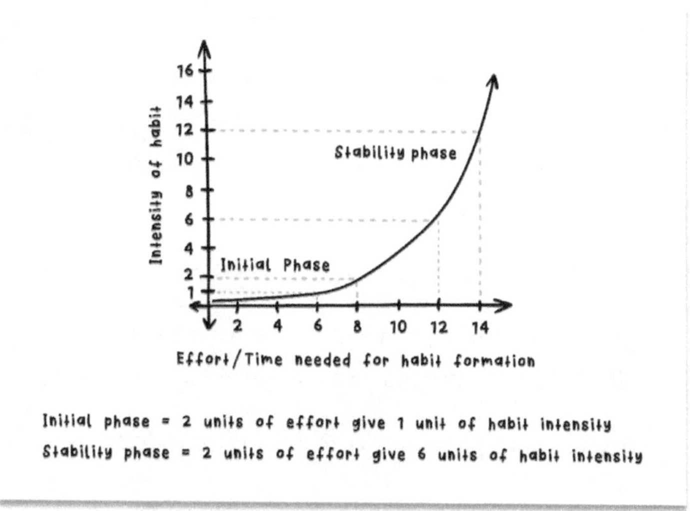

Pic 15: The initial phase of habit formation requires the maximum effort and attention.

In the initial phases, 2 units of effort produce only 1 unit of habit. However, as one spends more time consistently on the habit formation journey, the efficiency of habit formation improves.

When one reaches the stability phase, the same 2 units of effort now give 6 units of habit.

The magic starts happening after you've put in a total 8 units of effort/ time. It's like the light at the end of the tunnel. The take-off of an aeroplane is the trickiest and most energy-consuming phase of the flight. However, you spend much less fuel at the cruising altitude to maintain the flight. You get more for less fuel. Bigger bang for the buck!

As habits get ingrained and are on autopilot, the amount of time/ effort needed to sustain reduces, i.e., it becomes easier to maintain that habit.

When the habit is fully formed, it is called the 'stability phase'. At this point, the habit strength and automaticity are at maximum, and as time passes, the habit behaviour plateaus and maintains itself without much effort or thinking. Here one would effortlessly carry on with the habit, even if there was no injection of motivation.

The stability phase is also which is the most efficient stage. Your mental faculties are not occupied consciously with the habit, and your mind can focus on other productive processes. Perhaps creating one more good habit or trying a hand at a new hobby.

To extend this a bit, and to summarise, it requires effort to either:

1. Acquire a new habit by making deliberate choices,
2. To eliminate a habit that was acquired spontaneously.

Both the above cases require hard/difficult choices/decisions.

The big question: How do you know your habit is a 'Good' Habit?

Consistency: The Power of Accumulation; the benefits of Repetition

Before we talk more about the special 'Super-habit' called consistency, let's assume that all the terms like consistency, persistence, accumulation, and repetition fall within the same bucket, and we can collectively refer to them as 'Consistency'.

In this section, we will quote several examples from different spheres of life where consistency is key and drives the main outcome.

Example 1: The Daily Run

The simple example of running just 1 km a day consistently for 365 days would give us a far grander outcome than running 10 half marathons. Just 1 km a day would accumulate 365 km, and each km would be a breeze after you get into a daily habit.

So, your effort is very little per day, yet the outcome over a year is stunning. **Consistency creates results.**

Consistency reduces the amount of effort needed per unit of action after a habit is set in (**Pic 15**)

Example 2: The Camel's Back

Power of Consistent **Accumulation**

We have all heard the proverb, 'The last straw that broke the camel's back'. The farmer's camel keeps standing while his back is loaded with straw bundles. The farmer decides to load a bit more as the camel stands still. In his greed, he keeps adding small bits until the breaking point, and the camel collapses as soon as a single strand of straw is placed on its back.

This phrase is used in situations to denote culmination or decisive outcome, point of no return, pent-up emotions, etc. However, it also helps us appreciate the value of accumulation.

It is not that the last straw was the heaviest, which led to the camel's back being broken. It is the sum total of all the strands loaded before it. Each strand, individually weighing negligible yet accumulated in one place, consistently kept increasing the burden until the tipping point.

The same happens with good or bad habits. Our daily actions keep accumulating until the outcome starts manifesting; the habit becomes autopilot.

For anything good (or bad) to manifest, there must be accumulation, whether it is discipline, knowledge, sports or health regime, arts, and so on. **Accumulation creates momentum.**

Example 3: The Repetition Game

You must've seen priests in Temples, Mosques, Churches, and Monasteries rattling out lengthy holy verses effortlessly and non-stop, sometimes for hours together purely from memory. How did that perfection and ease come in?

Surely not by memorizing 10-15 times and then hoping it will remain like that throughout. No.

It is the outcome of frequently repeating the same not a hundred but thousands of times in different settings. Any glitches and lapses are corrected on the next attempt. And the cycle goes on.

Repetition helps reach an autopilot stage faster and creates perfection.

Here are some of the more famous and branded examples of incremental improvement, consistency, accumulation, persistence, and patience. You may want to search on your own on the internet.

- Usain Bolt's training schedule
- British Cycling Team: How it turned around the odds?
- Compound interest: How does it work?
- Bamboo tree: Why does it grow slowly?

Pic 16: Power of Consistent Accumulation

Coming back to the question of how long does one have to be consistent for something good to happen or a habit to form?

Popular belief says it takes about 21 days to make a habit or get some outcome from consistent behaviour. This number is more mythical than based on science.

Multiple observations across different studies show that the stability or plateau phase of a newly formed habit is achieved in about 16-17 weeks (average 66 days). Basically, this is the amount of time needed for that habit to become automatic.

Quite logically, it is also reported that tasks that are easy become habits more quickly. The chances of successful habit formation are also high if the tasks are PAD (Practical and Doable). The only condition is being consistent.

The journey itself during this period is as important as the milestone.

Interviews with patients and volunteers who successfully completed such studies show that one should frequently observe and aim for small wins. The participants should rejoice in the completion of that small daily target and take one day at a time.

And as small positive outcomes appear and are celebrated, repeating the tasks becomes progressively easier and more rewarding.

The only effort then is to provide a small pinch of motivation once in a while till the habit forms fully. If there is any larger role for willpower, then it is in maintaining a consistent streak. So, you will do very well if you just manage to have enough willpower to remain consistent for 60 to 70 days.

Coming back to the popular belief, even 21 days is a good start if you can continue it non-stop and repeat it **thrice.**

Big Question:

Two schools of thought: Isn't following a routine boring, even though you might be doing well? Should we change the setting?

Changing the scene, a bit, or the fruit or the juice, requires additional effort for the same output. As long as it doesn't come in the way of remaining consistent, a little variation may not harm.

Consistency itself is a Habit. A Super-Habit

The King of Habits

The Final word on Consistency and Habit

What we are going to talk about in this section may sound repetitive. And if it does, that's the intent.

Remember, repetition, accumulation, and consistency are the cornerstones of a successful habit-formation journey.

Consistency is the mother of Habits and the grandmother of Results.

Look at it as a chemical reaction, where you have an input raw material, you run the reaction, and after some time, you get outputs.

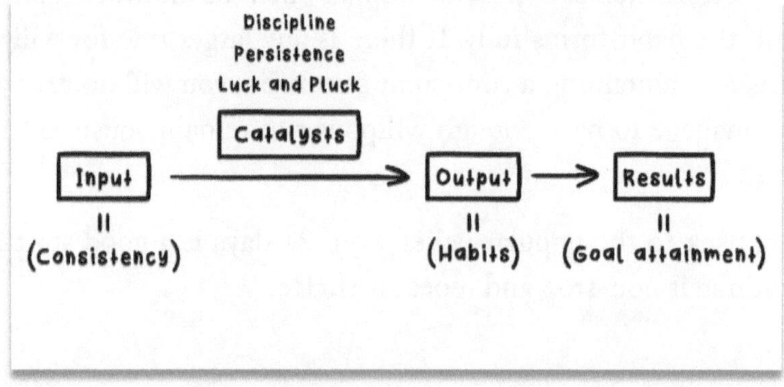

Pic 17: The Equation of Consistency to Results

Never forget the role of Luck and Pluck in outcomes.

Pluck: Intrinsic courage, intent, drive, and preparedness (through habit and consistency).

Luck: It is a random force of nature. But as someone wise mentioned, you get 'Lucky' when your preparation meets an opportunity.

So, fundamentally, if you have pluck, you can attract luck.

Start with a habit that is a PAD (Practical and Doable)

Secure your actions and goals with a PAD.

Ensure their success by PADing them up. An action that is PAD (Practical and Doable) and can be performed every day with minimal resistance. Every day until it becomes a habit.

If there is one Habit you want to form, let it be the habit of consistency.

In a way, consistency itself is a Habit. In fact, it is the most potent habit.

But it is a double-edged sword, though. You need to pulse-check what you are consistently at.

Is it arising out of easy choices or difficult decisions?

Difficult decisions lead to great habits.

So much so that the one thing that might influence human (or any other creature's) life could be its 'circle of habits'.

Consistency, Habit, and Outcome are rooted in Human Biology too.

Successful habit formation, whether a good or bad habit, is rooted in our Brain biology and is mediated via a number of Brain chemicals (hormones and neurotransmitters).

Four of these chemicals, namely Dopamine, Serotonin, Endorphins, and Oxytocin engage our nervous system in a complex yet coordinated manner to give rise to feelings of happiness, satisfaction, and contentment.

The level of these chemicals ebbs and flows in our body and brain depending on our activities and the outcome.

e.g., If we associate a high degree of fulfilment with our daily exercise routine, or to our ability to do generous charity or finish a task that has been pending for a long time, or being able to hang out with family, friends, and love interest, it will trigger a cascade of brain chemicals and leave us happy, proud, contended. These tasks, activities, and habits could be aligned with our value systems in different ways; hence, our biology would react according to how important they are to us. The above activities and pursuits, if repeated regularly, would continue to give us an injection of the happy/satisfaction chemicals.

Some of those then would turn into habits as we traverse the cycle of action, effect, habit, and result. Therefore, it is essential that we remember and possibly celebrate those small successes during the habit journey. Those small wins and repeats will cascade a virtuous cycle of habit formation and rewards.

The habit journey with brain chemicals

Action/Behaviour → Brain chemicals → mindfulness and realise the benefits → repeat behaviour → same benefits → positive addiction/ Consistency → Habit → Outcome/Results

Consistency is the King of Habits

The first and only habit someone needs to develop is the habit of consistency. Consistency is the key to habit formation. And habits beget outcomes.

In other words, if we want the outcome, make consistency/repetition your foremost and perhaps your **only** habit. Everything else will fit snugly into your life.

And when we are aware of what we are pursuing consistently, we can adopt or reject that behaviour or activity based on its potential impact on our larger goals.

If most habits were based on easy choices and decisions, they would only take us that far. Or perhaps keep us where we are.

Only relatively more difficult and uncomfortable choices give way to excellent and great habits. In turn, positive outcomes start showing up.

And the best thing is that Positive outcomes create space for more positive habits in other spheres of life.

> **People do not decide their futures, they decide their habits and their habits decide their futures.**
>
> **– F.M. Alexander**

How to increase your chances of being consistent

Being consistent in whatever one does is crucial for achieving goals and forming lasting habits. Here are a few strategies that can help:

1. **Start small:** Begin by setting small, achievable goals and focusing on consistency in the short-term. This will help to build momentum and confidence.
2. **Plan early:** Set specific, measurable, and action-oriented goals, and develop a plan for achieving them. Identify the steps you need to take and the resources you need to acquire in order to accomplish your goals.
3. **Track your progress:** Keep a record of your progress, either by writing it down or using a tracking app. This will help you stay motivated and celebrate your successes.
4. **Create a routine:** Establish a regular routine for completing your goals. Habits are most likely to form when the behaviour is performed at the same time and in the same place.
5. **Reward yourself:** Reward yourself for making progress. Give yourself positive reinforcement for completing your goals and meeting your milestones.
6. **Keep motivation high, but don't wait for it:** Remind yourself why you started and what you are working towards. Keep your motivation high by visualizing the end goal. Fall back on consistency when motivation wavers.
7. **Adjust as necessary:** Be flexible; if you find that something is not working, adjust your approach. Be open to trying new strategies and approaches.
8. **Be accountable:** Share your goals with a friend, family, or mentor and ask them to hold you accountable. This will make you more likely to follow through.
9. By following these strategies, you can increase your chances of being consistent and forming lasting habits. Remember, **consistency** is the key and small progress over time adds up to big results.

Pit Stop 2: Overcoming Some Decision Dilemma

Our choices directly impact the amount of Time or Money we eventually have. But it's not a direct transition, and neither is it immediate or sudden. It takes time, and sometimes it is so silent that we fail to notice until it is too late. Hence, we need to ask ourselves:

- Time: Money decision- How do you know your actions will generate more Time or Money?
- Easy: Difficult decision- How do you know whether the decision or choice you are taking is Easy or Difficult?
- Motivation: Consistency decision- How do you know whether you need Motivation or Consistency to get on with a task and finish what you started?

If you are a fan of 'motivation', remember that motivation succeeds only when there is MOTIVE, and there is ACTION hand in hand, consistently.

Motive without action and action without motive are equally useless.

The Brain Twister Tip:

If we are trying to find a good, clean excuse to procrastinate or justify not doing something, it is likely that it is the most difficult choice and hence probably the only one worth doing.

Logically if difficult choices create good habits and good habits create an easy life, then it is worth pursuing difficult choices. The question is how to make difficult choices easy. As an oxymoron, this book is a journey of making difficult choices easy to follow.

In the next chapter, let's start piecing the Jigsaw puzzle and see how our choices determine our overall state of mind and happiness.

The Bottomline

6. The Triangles of Life and the Happiness Formula

Happiness is being able to do what you had set out to do, no matter how small.

Have you ever wondered why one might be 'successful' yet feel unfulfilled?

I may have the best habits in the world and am making the most difficult choices and consistently following up on those, yet I am not happy. What's going wrong?

Having good habits and acquiring material success is one thing, but it may not still mean happiness and contentment.

Happiness, Contentment, and Satisfaction

One could ask, what would positive habits do for me except for making me realise my goals? Fair question.

Let's think about what each of those goals would do over a period of time. Would we stop after we reach a couple of goals?

Could it be that achieving a goal may not end our quest? What exactly is that quest which we are all pursuing without even knowing?

Let's start with the assumption (for some of us, it could be real) that the single most important goal or quest being pursued is **'Happiness/ Contentment'**.

The interesting thing about selecting this goal (or quest) is that it will test every hypothesis and trip about making decisions and leading a great life. It will make us take the various diagnostic tests which validate or trash our assumptions. It will make us climb up and down various 'decision trees' on the way.

It will be the true 'North Star' in our days and life.

Easier said than done.

How do we explain Happiness, Contentment, or Satisfaction to a 5-year-old?

Classically speaking, when you are happy, there is a sense of overall **well-being** and **fulfilment,** and you feel good about not only yourself but generally about others too. Essentially, you are content with what you have and perhaps **feel lucky** too. There is a sense of **gratitude** and **abundance** for things and social connections. All in all, you feel more **settled** within and outside of life and are on the **right track**. You are **in control of your time** and hence your money too.

The range of negative feelings that you may succumb to at other times is prominently absent when you are happy. In short, you are generally **satisfied** with your life.

Of course, the trigger could differ for different people based on what they value most. And that's why knowing what matters most to you and your potential is important. (Refer to the APE™ Triangle in Chapter 3)

These positive feelings of happiness, satisfaction and contentment are quite similar. It might be thus simpler to use **'Satisfaction'** as a representation of such positive emotions as Happiness and Contentment.

But before we proceed, it is important to differentiate between **Happiness vs Pleasure.**

As per a popular Indian thinker, the feeling of 'Pleasure' is short-term and shallow. It keeps you bound and hostage to desires, and hence you are not essentially free. 'Happiness', on the other hand, is when one is thankful for what is already there. You are full, content, and satisfied, and therefore grateful.

This sense of abundance and feeling of gratitude go hand in hand and therefore are an essential component of being in a state of happiness and satisfaction.

How to feel abundant? A quick tip.

Most would argue that happiness/contentment are perhaps linked directly and proportionally to access to money, power, privilege, social standing etc. It may certainly be true if we consider only the upper layers of the Happiness Hierarchy.

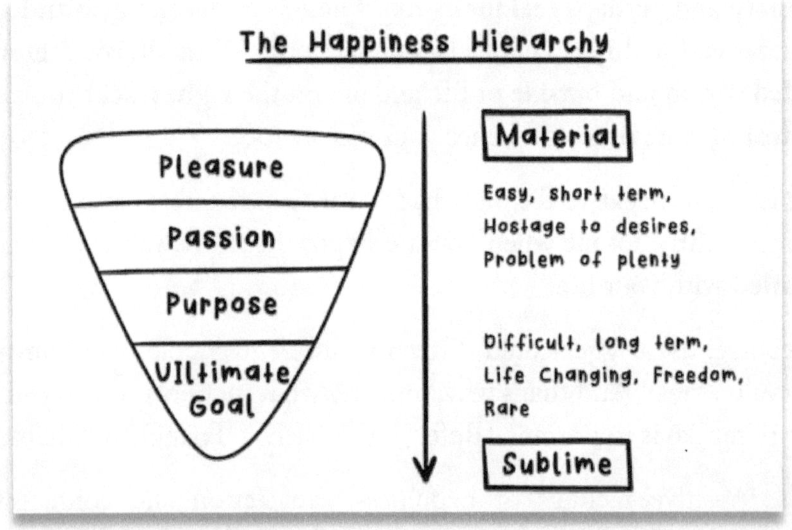

Pic 18: The Happiness Hierarchy

If you have enough money, power, and access, it is easy to 'feel' you are happy. However, that feeling may be more of a transient emotion, leaving you craving for more in a never-ending cycle. You would still wake up every day feeling deficient. Still feeling wronged, still having a FOMO (Fear Of Missing Out). Repeating all those pleasurable pursuits would still not 'keep' you happy. You will still not be content.

Contrast that, for example, with an active opportunity to do charity. We saw earlier that one of the pillars of happiness (aka satisfaction) is the sense of 'abundance'. Interestingly, most people view abundance in comparison to others around them. And therefore, abundance is not absolute; it is relative. One feels more, or less abundant depending on with whom they compare themselves.

We may be multi-millionaires and yet feel deficient and have FOMO depending upon how we view ourselves and our achievements in relation to others.

It is only when we start looking beyond our immediate circle and think about 'giving' that we realise our true net worth and value, both in terms of monetary and non-tangible possessions.

Imagine a child in an impoverished village struggling to reach school every day because he doesn't have a pair of slippers. Something that costs perhaps a dollar or two. The absence of those two dollars prevents him from getting a decent chance at consistent education. If he can afford a pair of slippers one day, he might feel like the luckiest or happiest person in the world. The value of that paltry sum is unimaginably high for him. It might make him feel abundant. One of the key pillars of happiness.

If two dollars can make someone feel lucky and abundant, it is quite perplexing why most of us with relatively higher access to wealth and resources should feel deficient.

There is something fundamentally wrong with how we might be viewing and using our access to wealth.

Is it possible that we find opportunities to convert a small amount of our resources into high-value, high-impact assets by simply 'giving'? Giving, where the moment the resource/asset changes hands, it rises astronomically in value. Those two dollars become a life-changing opportunity for someone else.

That, perhaps, is a way to feel abundant and happy.

BIG QUESTION:

Sense of Abundance

Have we ever thought about how money is different from wealth?

Wealth is far bigger and more global than money. **Wealth is the sense of abundance.**

Someone said wealth consists not in having great possessions but in having few wants. Counterintuitively it means that 'the less you want, the more you will feel you have'. And that feeling is a sure-shot direction towards abundance and happiness.

There may, of course, be more ways to happiness than only doing charity and feeling abundant or wanting less.

Maybe altering the way, we use our money. Perhaps spending some on materials but much more of it to buy Time.

Recall the Chapter 4, Time-Money equation. Let's think about those again. That may be another way of feeling abundant, the abundance of Time. And when you have a sense of control over your time, you tend to be quite happy.

Looking back at the Happiness hierarchy in the beginning of this chapter, the journey from consuming for pleasure to producing and giving opens the doors for a higher purpose, long-term happiness, and satisfaction.

And therefore, it is beyond doubt that a sustained state of happiness/ Satisfaction is life's biggest success. And it is not connected to any numerical value of wealth, resources, or access.

Instead, a proven path to happiness is placing your life in the APE™ Triangle and working towards bridging the gap between your Achievement, Potential, and Expectations. Satisfaction is then an outcome of your progress towards bridging that gap where all these three variables overlap seamlessly.

How does one reach that state of mind?

It is a layered process but quite logical. And as we saw in the last few pages, it would require us to be 'consistent' in our pursuit of the happiness goal.

And for that, Expectation management and knowing oneself intimately (and knowing one's true and practical capabilities) are paramount.

How does the APE triangle open up our path to happiness?

(Refer to the APE triangle in Chapter 3)

One of the biggest indicators of how happy we can be is our understanding of our own potential, our ability to manage expectations, and doing whatever is needed to achieve goals that are true to our potential. As long as these three variables are aligned, we should be quite happy.

Achievement: One can only achieve something with consistent habits and actions. You can rest assured that you will achieve 'something' if you are consistent.

Potential: Knowing oneself intimately is the single most important enquiry one could make. Being genuinely aware of our own current and future potential helps us have practical yet exciting expectations of ourselves.

Expectation: Intimate knowledge about ourselves and the awareness of our genuine constraints help us set our expectations and lead us to chase PAD (Practical and Doable) goals.

Understanding where we are currently in our APE triangle requires introspection. It shouldn't be rushed because if we figure it out well now, it will be a pleasant and uncluttered journey later. It starts with P and E and culminates with A.

P and **E** require thinking. It is like analysing what our Potential and Expectations from life are. Only when we can acknowledge the gap can we start towards the Action-oriented **A**.

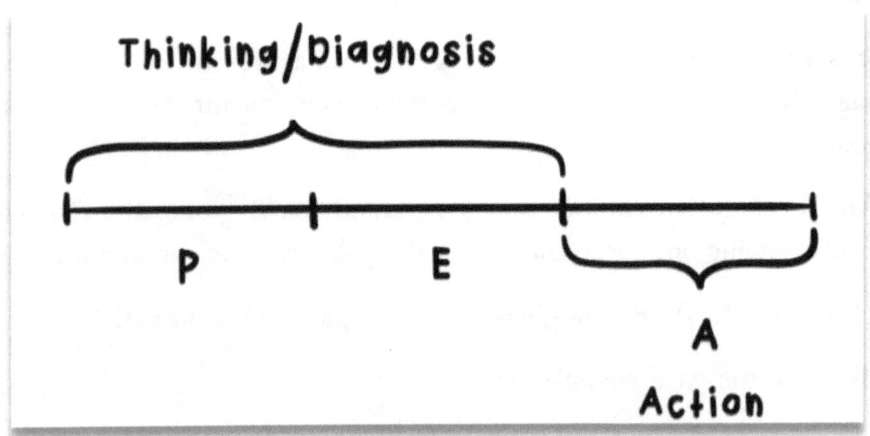

Pic 19: The Thinking and Action of the APE™ Triangle

The Thinking and Diagnosis phase is like sharpening the Axe. Action phase is like chopping the wood. Sharper the Axe, better the wood chips.

Here's how most people who have successfully gone through the exercise used it. Let's refresh the concept in the next text box.

In concept:

Step 1:

Bring Expectations (E) closer to P or raise the Potential (P) to match E. But remember, we are considering P to be generally fixed. The potential could be raised, but it would require additional efforts, commitment, exposure, upskilling etc.

Instead, in a given frame of time, the best way is to move E down to a reasonable level.

How?

Reduce Expectations by knowing ourselves better each day. If we can do that, we should be a bit closer to being at ease. This is a crucial step in **Expectation Management** and has a philosophical/spiritual tinge to it. This process is similar to sharpening the axe.

Step 2:

Now that our Expectations and Potential are aligned, i.e., our expectations of ourselves are reasonable and practical, there may still be a gap between our Expectations and Achievements.

The only way, then, is to reduce the gap between A and E.

How?

Increase A (Achievement) to be closer to P and E. This is **Pureplay Action** and on the ground, getting things done. This is the act of consistently chopping the wood with a sharp axe. This will ensure achieving what you are capable of and what you've committed and are expected to do.

Step 3:

At this stage, your Achievements and Expectations are aligned, and you are operating at your true potential. You now need to maintain the momentum through awareness, consistency, and persistence.

Strive actively to keep A close to P and sustain it as per your expectations.

That's your Ideal/Satisfied Triangle. That's what you started the journey for.

In Practice:

Thinking and Diagnosis Phase (Knowing your E and P)

Step 1: Expectation

Assume (for the purpose of expectation setting) that Potential is constant and fixed. Now honestly assess what your potential is (for a certain target) and how far you have reached in it.

- Ask whether the expectations/goals you have for yourself are fair and practical. One way to get the answer is to know exactly what needs to be invested from your side to ensure those expectations are met. Do you know how hard or easy those requirements are, and how much are you prepared to put in?
- **The Smile Test**: Imagine yourself working towards those goals, day in and out. Do the thoughts of the journey towards meeting those expectations put a 'smile' on your face? Would you feel the same positivity about the expectations even if you failed many times? Would you still smile and carry on?

If the answer to the **Smile Test** is still YES, you may indeed have a fair expectation from yourself. Otherwise, think very hard, tone down your expectations, and retake the smile test.

Step 2: Potential

The immediate next step would be to scrutinise your **potential**, depending on whether the answer to the Smile question is YES or NO.

- If the answer to the Smile question in Step 1 is **YES**, then see whether your potential (i.e., capability, willingness to learn, unlearn and relearn) is enough to support your expectations and goals.
- Be very practical when you assess your potential. Retake the smile test and see if you are equally enthused when you are brutally honest about your true capabilities and resilience.

- Take the test again 2-3 times more in as many days.
- If the answer is still YES, your Expectations and Potential are perhaps in sync.
- You may then want to start your journey towards Achievement. We will talk more about it in a bit.

Let's now see if the answer to the Smile question in Step 1 is **NO**. That generally means that you might be expecting a bit too much, perhaps too soon from yourself. If the prospect of the journey to meet those expectations doesn't excite you and instead takes energy away from you, it's better to reassess your expectations.

- It may be the right time to tone the expectations down to the point of your true potential. Imagine meeting your toned-down expectations by putting in the efforts and skills that you are confident of. Keep observing when the expectations and goals feel doable, and you feel relieved.
- Do you feel like smiling and feel satisfied with the possibility of meeting the 'new' expectations?

At this stage, look at the APE diagrams again and identify which triangle you relate to. The Baseline APE triangle or the Satisfied APE triangle. You may discover that you are very close to being satisfied, and there is hardly any gap between your 'genuine' Expectation and Potential. Believe me, that's a great place to be. Refer to Chapter 3.

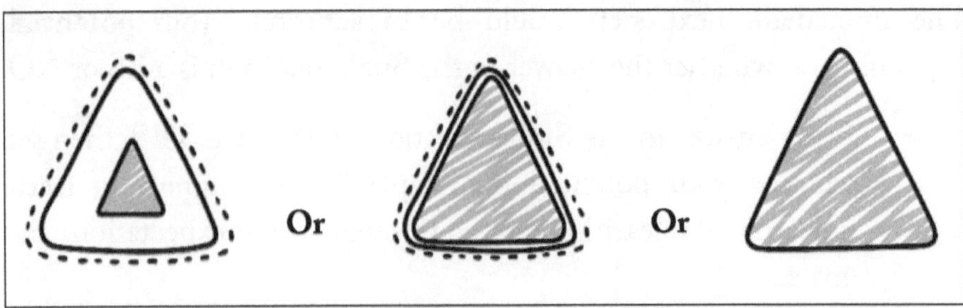

It may also turn out that your Potential and Expectations are aligned, but you need to cover a visible gap in Achievement.

Now hold that thought and get into Action mode to crack the Achievement code.

Action Phase (Doing A)

Step 3: Achievement

Whatever your answer to the Smile test, once your Expectation and Potential are aligned, it's time to chase the action-driven Achievement code. The key assumption is that your Achievement triangle is smaller than your Potential and Expectation triangle. In other words, you are not operating at your full potential.

1. First, analyse and agree on **what** is stopping you from 'Achieving your full potential' and what is currently deficient in your life; Time, Money, or both.

   - Probe the daily 'decisions or choices' you make. (For reference, check Pit Stop 1 and Chapter 5)
   - Are those choices acting as 'Roadblocks' or 'Enablers' towards your achievements/goals?
   - Are those choices contributing towards your deficiencies in either Time or Money? e.g., quick fix and easy choices/habits robbing you of your disposable time?

2. Identify and agree on a Goal or Action to remove the roadblocks. Let's say 'carving out 2 hours' from your day and investing in yourself towards working on that Goal/Action.

   - The goal should be such that, if met, it should bring your Achievements closer (either directly or indirectly) to your potential. (Look at the APE Triangle again)
   - Remember, this time, the approach towards the 'chosen goal' should differ from your earlier attempts.
   - Different in what way? You must understand and build a relationship with your Choices, Decisions, Habits, Motivation, and Willpower. You need to ask and

- remind yourself all too often, **what am I prepared to do CONSISTENTLY without getting bogged down by an occasional miss?**
- **Etch it in your subconscious that consistency is the only and only way towards** sustained results and desired outcomes. In short, to achieve that 'goal'.
- **And Achieving Goals aligned with our true Potential and Expectation in life is a certain way to 'Happiness'.**

One could approach happiness not only by meditation and calmness, but it could be anything which clearly defines the purpose, removes distractions, builds enabling habits and puts you on the path to realise that state of mind called happiness.

While we work through the dynamics of the APE triangles, we also need to keep an eye on the T-M (Time and Money equation) and the Time-Money-Satisfaction balance, TMS (Chapter 3).

Eventually, if we must realise a certain level of life satisfaction we need:

- To play with the 2 all-powerful levers, Time, and Money.
- Understand our APE triangle intimately.
- Commit to Goals (PAD) and act according to our true potential and reasonable expectations.
- Take actions that are in line with our goals and are born out of difficult choices.
- Commit to Consistency (CTC), repeat the actions, and notice the incremental benefit and progress towards our goals.
- Repeat until these become habits, second nature.

By this time, we should be very close to realizing your goals and filling up our Achievement Triangle.

Let us test it in the next chapter, which is pretty much the "proof of the pudding".

Plato believed a happy person is one who **has principles and sticks to them**. He or she uses and practices these principles in order to become a **better person** and a **better member of society**.

And one who sticks to principles consistently ends up being happy…

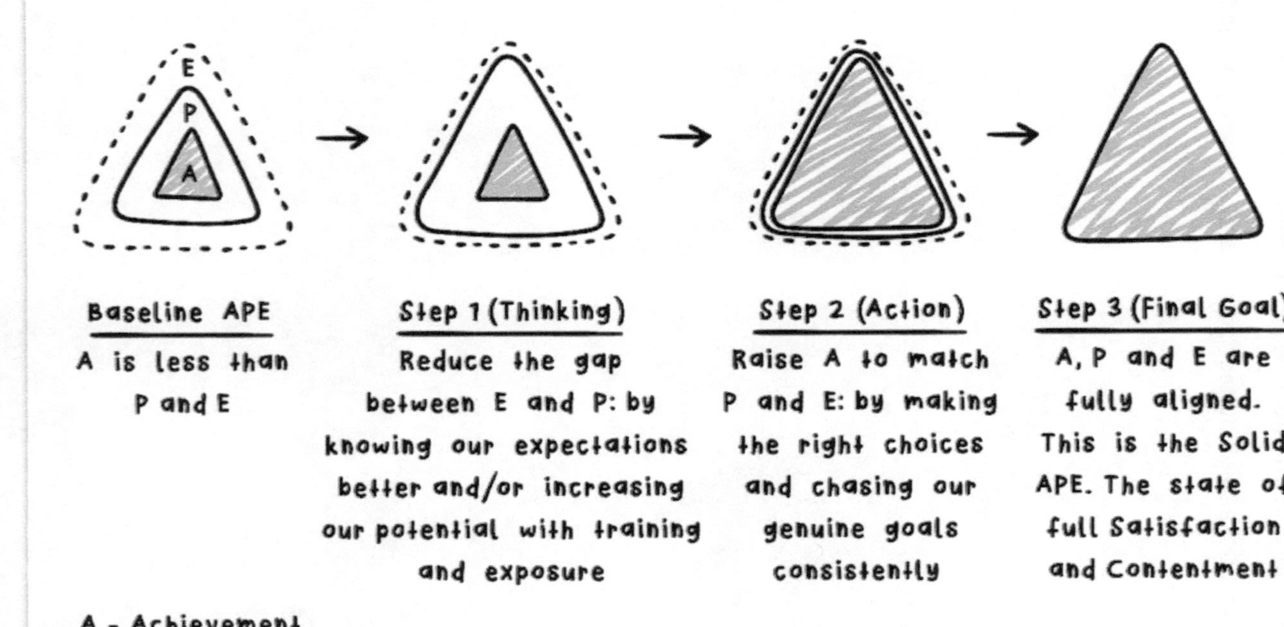

The journey of our Baseline APE™ to the Solid APE™
E
P
A
Baseline APE
A is less than P and E
Step 1 (Thinking)
Reduce the gap between E and P: by knowing our expectations better and/or increasing our potential with training and exposure
Step 2 (Action)
Raise A to match P and E: by making the right choices and chasing our genuine goals consistently
Step 3 (Final Goal)
A, P and E are fully aligned. This is the Solid APE. The state of full Satisfaction and Contentment
A - Achievement
P - Potential
E - Expectations

PART E

---

3 Weeks to Happiness

7. The 21-day Eureka: 3 Weeks to Happiness

Now that we have learned the concepts and seen examples of how Time, Money, Satisfaction, and Consistency play out, let's test those in our real life. And the one who can make that happen is only YOU. And I say that with a fair degree of confidence since you've already gone through the pages thus far, and perhaps, read and reread some of the passages with rapt attention.

In this chapter, we wouldn't boil the ocean but would pick only a few **target goals** and commit to achieving those, at the least.

The question is not HOW you would achieve the goal, but WHEN you would do that. When would you start in a way that it gets done once and for all? It is that simple when you decide.

Let's call it the **21 day Eureka**.

We will give ourselves 21 days to focus on just 'doing something'. Then another 21 days to continue doing while measuring and enjoying the small wins, the impact of consistency, and revel in seeing a new habit form.

For the final 21 days, we will continue the habit until we are confident that it has become so effortless that unless we do it, we are not at ease.

These 63 days (or 2 months) might be exactly what you needed to change the **APE™ triangle** in your favour.

Consider the phases to be like flying an Aeroplane from Taxiing the plane on the Tarmac to Take-off, then autopilot cruise, maintaining the altitude, and finally landing safely at your target location.

Phase 0: 'Planning and preparation'. Taxiing on the Tarmac

Phase 1: 21 days of focused 'Doing'. Take-off

Phase 2: 21 days of 'Maintenance and Measurement'. Autopilot Cruise and maintaining altitude

Phase 3: Repeat at least 21 days until fully ingrained as a Habit. Safe landing at Target location.

Before starting the journey (let's call it Phase 0), we must **choose our target habit.**

Phase 0: Taxiing on the Tarmac

'Planning and preparation'

1. Note down 3 habits you want to build (or stop in case of a bad habit).

    a. Use the **Utility filter** (how useful the habit/action will be). **Refer to the Appendix for some filled examples and blank templates for use.**

2. Ask yourself if it is possible to measure the output and ascertain whether you are on track and making a progress.

3. Decide the 'what' parameter you will measure as an output for each. e.g., you may say you want to be more generous, but how do you define generosity daily? Put a number on it.

    Use the table below to document the 3 habits in descending order of utility. Calculate utility by using the **Utility filter.**

No.	Goal/Habit	Detail	Target	What will I measure?
1				
2				
3				

Now let's move on to selecting only 1 out of the 3. How?

Give the list a hard look and convince yourself which one you are **prepared to CONSISTENTLY do without getting bogged down by an occasional miss.**

Pick that **one habit** that you feel:

i. Is the most valuable as per the **utility filter/score.**

ii. Is the most likely to withstand the roadblocks of illness, waning interest, holidays, distractions, procrastination etc.

iii. Will get social support with reminders and encouragement.

iv. You are absolutely committed to remaining consistent.

v. Is not dependent on others, and if need be, you can walk the path alone.

Here's just an example. (You need to do your own).

No.	Goal/Habit	Detail	Target	What will I measure?
1	Forming a habit of running every day	Slow jogging or running in the open air in the morning and evening	At least 2km in 15 to 20 mins	Number of days I could meet the target in a week

That's the end of Phase 0.

By this time, you should be perfectly clear about a goal that you are chasing. It might be a habit you want to form, or a habit you want to get rid of, and finally, getting something done which you've been procrastinating.

Phase 1: Take-off

21 days of focused 'Doing'.

1. Start by putting the target prominently at places where it reminds you of what you've committed to doing and what it would look like after you've achieved it. Make it read and sound exciting.

   e.g., Instead of simply putting "I want to lose 10 pounds", try writing, "I want to feel 10 years younger" or "All my old clothes should fit me again", and so on.

   e.g., Instead of simply saying, "I want to regularly do charity", why not "I want to feel abundant and useful" or "I want to sleep with a smile on my face"?

Something useful some of my mentees have done is to make a **'Commitment Charter'.**

Example:

Commitment Charter	
Target →	
Why am I doing this?	I want for a daily habit that will help me in other health goals like losing weight
When would I stop (Final output after 63 days)?	Until jogging/ walking 2 kms becomes my daily habit
How do I monitor myself? →	
Who do I go for help when offtrack?	
1. 2. 3.	
Why I can't afford to miss it? →	
Ask yourself, have I missed a few times? What made me miss? What can I do to avoid missing in future?	
How am I doing at the end of 30 days (output)?	70% times I am meeting my daily target; Lost 3 kgs; Feeling proud
How am I doing at the end of 50 days (output)?	85% times I am meeting my daily target; Lost 3 kgs; Feeling great
How am I doing at the end of 63 days (output)?	Jogging every day is my Habit now. I feel something's not right if I miss even for a single day.
The Key question. Have I been CONSISTENT? →	My Honest answer:
70-80% compliance is success. Project it over 365 days. Work out the simple math of number of days missed. You are allowed to change the target only 1 time, within the first 15 days.	

2. Start the 21-day cycle. This is only the Input phase.

3. Keep looking at the Commitment Charter occasionally. However, avoid the temptation of measuring the final output yet.

4. The core objective of this 21 days phase is to remain consistent, at least to the level that we have committed ourselves. e.g., 70% compliance means going for a jog of 5 days out of 7 days per week.

   a. Always target 100%, BUT a deliberate and planned compliance of 75% and above should also be a matter of pride.

   b. Celebrate that win as you prepare to enter Phase 2.

Practical tip in this phase:

1. Remind yourself that you had to start somewhere, and this is that 'somewhere'.

2. Share the plan with the people who really care about your win.

3. Develop a 'daily routine' to dedicate time to your chosen target.

4. The steps won't become easy on their own. Instead, arrange things around yourself so that 'taking the next step' is convenient.   In other words, how do you 'reduce the friction' so that the next steps are smooth?

   • What about the night before, keeping your shoes, socks, and jogging shorts ready on the chair (that you sit on the first thing you get up in the morning)?

   • What about keeping a glass, a slice of lemon, and a thermos-flask of warm water next to your nightstand?

5. Every 7-10 days of continuous and consistent performance, daydream about how it would be when your final goal is met.

6. Remember: Discipline and Regret are both painful. Decide what you want to live with.

Phase 2: Autopilot Cruise and maintaining altitude

21 days of 'Maintenance and Measurement'.

1. Measure the incremental benefits which are directly related to your input/efforts. It is progress, whether in input or the intended output.
2. Ensure that you are at least 70-80% sticking to the target in the Commitment Charter.
3. Continue the journey with pride and enthusiasm.
4. Visualise how great it would feel when you meet the target, and this becomes a Habit.

Practical tip in this phase:

1. Don't worry about the outcome yet. Just focus on getting by each step, each day.
2. Treat it as a jigsaw puzzle. Keep moving the small pieces, one at a time, but consistently.
3. Ask your loved ones to remind you if they see you becoming inconsistent in your daily commitments.
4. Once in a while, look back and compare where you started and where you are already in terms of the new habit.

Phase 3: Safe landing at the Target location

Repeat at least 21 days until fully ingrained as a Habit.

1. Repeat till it becomes a strong habit, and you can be 75-80% compliant over a period of 21-day blocks.
2. Be aware of whether missing your target on a day or two bothers you or not. Ideally, when a habit is formed, it should feel uncomfortable when you miss it even once.

Practical tip in this phase:

1. Remind yourself of the main goals and, more importantly, the steps that make up the goal.

2. Ask yourself whether what you are doing (at any moment) is worth it.

3. Say NO at least once a week. NO to things that are likely to distract you from your goal. It will leave you with more time to yourself and your goals.

4. Give things away. That's one way of feeling abundant.

5. Organise your home and surroundings. A neat home = A neat mind = Clear focus on goals.

6. Keep things handy which are needed for your next task. Prepare beforehand to 'reduce the friction'.

7. If a task takes 2 mins or less, do it right away.

8. Be honest with yourself. That's all that matters.

Try this, and you won't regret it!

8. Afterword and Final Thoughts

On one of my European trips, I met a French gentleman, a timber merchant. He also finds mention in my Travel Adventure book, "Time Travel: To the Edge of History". I found him as one of the most energetic, busy, and yet a satisfied person I have interacted with face to face.

Amongst many things we discussed, one was about the power of focus and perseverance. He said, "I do many things and enjoy those. But there is ONE thing that I do as if my life depends on it. Like breathing, every moment, every day without fail. If I stop, I die".

This he meant to be his hobby of tending to his terrace garden, each pot at a time, and practising the art of Bonsai. This also means that he needs to be up at 6 am every morning to take an hour from his schedule to be among the plants. He aims to do a YouTube series on 100 Bonsai plants that can be grown in France.

According to him, he focused on that ONE big habit that would take him to his goal of 100 Bonsai plants. That habit was getting up at 6 am every day, consistently.

That plane journey had gotten me thinking about the ONE big habit that I needed, to realise the goals I had been pushing out for some years now. Three months later, I had homed in on that one habit, in fact, two.

I decided to write at least 400 to 600 words EVERY DAY. No matter how the words came out or whether they made much sense for the debut book I was targeting. The goal was only to build the habit of writing every day.

My second habit was to go for a run twice a day, without fail, even if it meant for a mere kilometre.

For 45 to 60 days, the content didn't matter; I was focused only on consistency. Just DOING it mattered.

Let's do it together. Let us decide 4 things right here on these pages. The only condition is that you should do those 'consistently'. Call them 'goals or habits' if you must.

I will suggest three, and you fill in one. Begin with something which you can control better.

Let's see where we land. Do refer to the pages above on the 21-day Eureka exercise.

1. The Habit of Eating Dinner every day between 7-8 pm and then going for a 2 km walk

2. The Habit of Consistency (Do whatever you do, but do it CONSISTENTLY)

3. The Habit of Expectation Management (Keep Your Expectations Close to Your Potential)

4. ____

   (fill in your own goal/habit)

Let yourself go through the full commitment cycle, completion, and results for these small nuggets. Your brain would want to repeat those because completion feels good.

No harm in repeating.

If one habit could be called the 'King of habits', the Super-habit, it would be 'Consistency'. If you have the habit of consistency, you are unbeatable. You will finish what you start, undoubtedly.

And if there was one *"Guru Mantra"* (the closest equivalent to 'Gospel Truth') ever, that would be consistency.

Do whatever, do it consistently every day. Be it…

1. Stretch every 10 mins
2. Tend to the plants
3. Drink lemon water
4. Take a walk
5. Breathe deeply
6. Simply run, alone if needed.

Make Consistency your Habit and that habit your goal.

The habit of consistency turned around the fortunes of Aneela and transformed her into Karishma.

Her consistent work on Expectation management. Her consistent focus on the Time-Money equation. Her consistent enquiry on the choices she was making daily and her consistent reminder that Easy Choices make Difficult Lives and Difficult Choices create Easy Lives.

At the end of the day, Karishma lives on and thrives on those moments of consistent choices and habits.

Her next target is to choose an exquisite dress for her award ceremony. Perhaps a handwoven Sambalpuri Silk Saree from the Cooperative handloom, which she adopted as a sponsor a year back.

Some like the journey, and some like the destination.

The one who likes the destination shouldn't care about a comfortable journey. The one who likes the journey doesn't need to wait for the destination. In the end, we all win if we know who we are and what we really like.

Appendix: Cheat Sheet and Tools for the Book

If you have to remember **6 concepts**:

- **Circle of Control diagram:** For all the time in the world, we control only a very small portion of that. So, let's use it judiciously.
- **Time-Money equation:** Time and Money are interchangeable currencies. You can spend one to buy the other.
- **APE™ Triangle:** The alignment of your true Potential, Expectations, and Achievements is the most important step towards happiness.
- **ECDL-DCEL:** Easy Choices lead to Difficult Life, and Difficult Choices lead to an Easy life. Choose wisely.
- **Consistency → Habits → Outcomes:** Consistency is the mother of habits and grandmother of outcomes (Results).
- **PAD:** Starting with Practical and Doable small steps leads to a longer and more consistent journey.

If you have to follow **6 tips**:

- Prioritise your Time over Money. Rest will fall in place.
- The best way to spend money is to buy more time with it.
- Know your True Potential; Set reasonable Expectations and then go all out to achieve those.
- Given 2 choices, pick the one that seems to be more difficult.
- Never rely on motivation alone. It can come and go. Stick to consistency for results.
- Habits may take anywhere between 10 to 200 days to firmly establish. Take the 21-day exercise (Chapter 7) and follow through. You will surprise yourself.

If you have to use **4 templates** to apply to yourself.

- Time-Money graphs
- APE™ Triangle
- Utility Filter
- Commitment Charter

The golden rules and words to remember:

- Organise your home and surroundings. A neat home = A neat mind = Clear focus on goals.
- Remember the Circle of Control diagram.
- If you have to follow 3 golden terms: Choice and Commitment to Consistency (CCC).
- Commitment to consistency is the true wealth.
- The only habit that ever mattered was consistency. Everything else follows.
- In the pursuit of habit formation, put progress before perfectionism.
- Habit formation **>** Goal formation. When habits are formed, goals become easy.
- Always visualise how great it would feel when you meet the target, and this becomes a habit.
- Motivation is what you get when you strike a matchstick. It helps you light up a candle before withering away. That candle is the consistent source of light you wanted, and you get.
- Consistency **>** Motivation
- Instead of simply saying, *"I want to regularly do charity regularly"*, *why not "I want to feel abundant and useful" or "I want to sleep with a smile on my face"*.
- If you can manage your expectations, you can manage your life and happiness.
- Lesser you want, the more you will feel you have.
- Take smile test (Chapter 6)

- Feeling Lucky and Abundant is not that difficult. Give things away. That's one way of feeling abundant.
- Discipline and Regret, both are painful. Decide what you want to live with.
- There is no bigger success than happiness and contentment.
- Be Consistent to be happy
- Celebrate

And before we sign off, here are some basic tips on habit formation, with a simple example of a daily exercise routine adapted from a blog by the author Leo Babauta.

You may take what you want from it and leave the rest, as long as you are retaining the part of being **consistent.**

1. **Set a time.** Decide whether you're more likely to stick with it in the morning or lunchtime or evening and stick with that time. I've set the time of 5:30 am every day, and I'm trying my best not to vary from that time. If you don't set a time, you're more likely to put it off until you have more time or energy and then put it off until the next day. Soon, it's not a habit at all.

2. **Send yourself a reminder.** I use Memo to Me, but there are several ways to send yourself an email or text reminder, so you'll never forget. Then, when you get the reminder, do it right away. Don't brook any delays.

3. **Start small.** This is perhaps the most useful suggestion of all. When I start exercising, I always start with lots of energy, enthusiasm, and ambition. I think I can do more than I can. However, doing too much, at the beginning leads to burnout, which leads to quitting your habit. When you first try to make exercise a daily habit, chances are, your body won't be used to that kind of stress. The key is to do only 20 minutes in the beginning and do it nicely and easily. Nothing hard. Even 10-15 minutes is fine at first if you're just starting out. What is important is to get out there, getting your body used to daily exercise slowly, and forming that habit.

4. **Progress later**. Once your body is used to daily exercise, you can slowly start to increase the amount and intensity of your exercise. Wait at least two weeks before starting to increase — that's the minimum your body needs to adjust. Once it begins to feel way too easy, you can start increasing the length of your workouts to 30 and then 40 minutes, and eventually up to an hour. Once you do that, you can gradually increase the intensity — running faster or harder, for example. Try not to increase both distance and intensity at the same time.

5. **Make it pleasurable**. If you associate a habit with pain, you will shy away from it. But if it's fun, you'll look forward to doing it. That's why I've been focusing on pleasure in this beginning stage of my new habit. I go slowly, enjoying the scenery, the fresh morning air, the beautiful sky as the sun rises, and the quiet time of solitude and contemplation. It's actually something I enjoy doing. An MP3 player with some great music helps.

6. **Lay out your gear**. The fewer obstacles and less friction in forming your new habit, the more likely you are to be successful. If you have to wake up early and get a bunch of gear together while half awake, you might just want to go back to bed. But if you lay out your workout clothes and shoes and watch and mp3 player or whatever you need for your exercise, you'll be ready to go with no friction at all.

7. **Just head out the door**. My rule is to get my running shoes on and out the door. I don't worry about how long I have to go or how hard it will be. Just get out and get started. Once you've done that, it's a piece of cake.

8. **Mix it up**. One thing I like about triathlon training is that daily exercise isn't boring — instead of running every day, now I've got a variety of sports to do, making it much more interesting. But perhaps just as important is that I'm using different muscles for each sport, especially swimming. Sure, some of the same muscles are used, but they're used differently with different stresses on them. What that means is that I'm not pounding the

same muscles every day. That gives them a chance to recover because, without recovery, you're just breaking your muscles down over and over.

9. **Have a relative rest day**. Again, recovery is very important, which is why you must give your body a chance to rest. If you're taking it easy and only doing 20 minutes, you should be OK without rest days. But it's still good to have one day of rest where you're not doing the same exercises as the other six days. You don't want to skip the day completely because then you're not consistent with your habits. That's why I do one day of strength training, where I don't use the same muscles as swimming, biking, and running. If you need more rest, you could just do 20 minutes of walking or even just a meditation session. The key is to do something every day, preferably something that gets you moving (meditation isn't the best example, but at least you'll be doing something) and keeps your habit formation going.

10. **Don't skip a day**. It's easy to say, "No problem, I've been doing it for five days … I'll just skip today". But that will make your habit formation harder. Consistency is key, so try not to skip a single day. If you do, don't beat yourself up, don't judge, don't feel bad — everyone messes up sometimes, and habit formation is a skill that requires practice. Start your 30-day challenge over again, try to identify the obstacle that led to your skipping a day, and prepare for it this time.

Utility Filter templates: Please use as guidance and example for tracking your own journey.

Starting a GOOD Habit-1		
Observe the choice I made, or decision I took, or the action I am doing, or the habit I am pursuing. Will it in future…	e.g. making sure that I go for a light jog everyday at least once for 15-20 mins. Atleast 9 out of 10 days. If it rains, I will spot jog at home.	Put your score below Yes=5 Maybe=3 No=0
Generate more Money	0	
Generate better physical health/Stamina/Resilience	5	
Generate more Resources	0	
Generate better relationships	3	
Generate more Quality of life	3	
Generate more peace of mind	3	
Bring Satisfaction and sense of achievement	3	
Create a better environment and harmony	0	
Create a better environment	5	
Create a Sense of Abundance	3	
Create more disposable TIME	3	
Total	28	
Any score more than 20, I should just go ahead and test it out for 20-40 days.		

Starting a GOOD Habit-2		
Observe the choice I made, or decision I took, or the action I am doing, or the habit I am pursuing. Will it in future...	e.g. Starting a structured charity or giving time to a social cause	Put your score below Yes=5 Maybe=3 No=0
Generate more Money	0	
Generate better physical health/Stamina/Resilience	3	
Generate more Resources	3	
Generate better relationships	5	
Generate more Quality of life	3	
Generate more peace of mind	3	
Bring Satisfaction and sense of achievement	3	
Create a better environment and harmony	5	
Create a better environment	5	
Create a Sense of Abundance	5	
Create more disposable TIME	3	
Total	38	

Any score more than 20, I should just go ahead and test it out for 20-40 days.

Stopping a BAD Habit		
Observe the choice I made, or decision I took, or the action I am doing, or the habit I am pursuing. Will it in future...	e.g. making sure that I wouldn't spend more that 30 mins on Netflix OR Social media in a day	Put your score below Yes=5 Maybe=3 No=0
Generate more Money	3	
Generate better physical health/Stamina/Resilience	3	
Generate more Resources	3	
Generate better relationships	3	
Generate more Quality of life	3	
Generate more peace of mind	3	
Bring Satisfaction and sense of achievement	3	
Create a better environment and harmony	0	
Create a better environment	5	
Create a Sense of Abundance	5	
Create more disposable TIME	5	
Total	36	
Any score more than 20, I should just go ahead and test it out for 20-40 days.		

Treat time as your biggest asset and consistency as your biggest habit.

Consistency is the real 'Super-habit'.

References

1. The Human Brain in Numbers: A Linearly Scaled-up Primate Brain, Frontiers in Human Neuroscience by Suzana Herculano-Houzel (2009).
2. The Role of Luck in Economic Success and Failure by Robert Frank and Philip Cook (1995).
3. Luck and Success: How Randomness Affects Our Lives by Richard Wiseman (2013).
4. Consistency in Habit Formation: An Analysis of Self-Reported Behaviours and Outcomes by Jackie Andrade and Philip G. Mayers, Journal of Applied Social Psychology (2011).
5. The Role of Goal Setting in the Formation of Habits by Benjamin Harkin and Neil Morris, Journal of Applied Social Psychology (2017).
6. The Price of Time: The Interconvertibility of Time and Money by Yoram Bauman and Elaina Rose (2015).
7. The Interconvertibility of Time and Money: A Study in the Relationship between Time and Money by K.M. Kosterev and E.V. Kostereva (2011).
8. The Interconvertibility of Time and Money: A Study in the Valuation of Time in Economic Analysis by John E. Roemer (1988).
9. The Interconvertibility of Time and Money: An Empirical Investigation by Peter G. Warr and J.C. Wilmshurst (1979).
10. The Luck Factor: The Scientific Study of the Lucky Mind by Richard Wiseman (2003).
11. The Role of Luck in Life Satisfaction and Well-Being by Stefan Schulz-Hardt and colleagues (2013).

12. A Longitudinal Field Study on the Role of Self-Control in Habit Formation, titled How to Form Good Habits, Front. Psychol? by Anouk van der Weiden and colleagues (2020).

13. The Consistency of Personality: A Study Across Five Countries by Wiebke Bleidorn and colleagues (2013).

14. Happiness and the Consistency of Positive and Negative Affect by Ed Diener and colleagues (1991).

15. The Benefits of Emotional Consistency: A Study of Longitudinal Change in Emotional Consistency and Life Satisfaction by Brett Ford and colleagues (2018).

16. Consistency of Happiness Across Situations and Over Time by Ed Diener and colleagues (1999).

17. The Habit Loop: How to Create New Habits That Stick by Charles Duhigg (2012).

18. Building Habits: A Framework for Developing Good Habits that Stick by James Clear (2018).

19. Creating New Habits: A Meta-Analysis of Habit Formation in Adults by Michael J. Wood, Jeffrey M. Quinn, and Wendy R. Wood (2009).

20. Habit Formation and Change in Adult Life by G. Alan Marlatt and Judith R. Gordon, Journal of Consulting and Clinical Psychology (1985).

21. How are habits formed: Modelling habit formation in the real world by Phillippa Lally and colleagues, European Journal of Social Psychology (2009).

22. Take the stairs by Rory Vaden.

23. https://7summitpathways.com/blog/four-levels-of-happiness/

24. https://zenhabits.net/how-to-make-exercise-a-daily-habit-with-a-may-challenge/

The references for the book can be found in various academic journals such as, The Journal of Economic Psychology, The Journal of Economic Literature, Journal of Economic Theory, and Journal of Economic Behaviour and Organization, and books and blogs published on the various topics.

Credits and Acknowledgements

1. Cover Design by Neha Gupta De
2. Images and graphs by Peeu Roy

In addition to the invaluable support that Neha and Peeu provided, there have been several individuals, friends and mentors who helped in the research, proof reading and critiquing the content from time to time, and even up to a couple of hours just before going to print.

They are the people who prove that every word written in the book can be lived by. They are the supermen and women, who personify the saying, "A busy (wo)man has time for everything".

Thank you, Kathleen, Bhaas, Himanshu Verma, Brahmananda Ghosh, Mitesh Patel for your support and ideas during the manuscript and editing phases.

My deep gratitude to Dr. Bibek Debroy, Dr. Anand Ranganathan, Ms. Nirupama Kotru, IAS. Member of Parliament Mr. Swapan Dasgupta, Mr. Ashish Dehade, Dr. Colleen Lightbody (Master Coach), Mr. Melvin D Paul, Mr. Pareekh Jain, Prof. Shanti Pappu, Ms. Shashikala Menon, Mr. Ashish Anand, Mr. Krishnan Iyer and Mr. Pradeep Shanbhag, for sharing their feedback and words of encouragement for the book.

A big reason for me becoming an author is my spirited father who despite being an Octogenarian believes he is barely half that age. Both my parents' reading and writing habits rubbed off well on me. And of course, Neha, my wife, and my daughter Nayonika who have promised me that they would be my biggest readers and would create a movement out of the book and the APE™ concept.

May we all be a bunch of Happy APEs.